the

PALEO

diet

the PALEO *diet*

FOOD YOUR BODY IS DESIGNED TO EAT

DANIEL GREEN

PHOTOGRAPHY BY CLARE WINFIELD

KYLE BOOKS

For Harry Charlie Green

A love that lasts forever

Published in 2015 by Kyle Books
www.kylebooks.com
general.enquiries@kylebooks.com

10 9 8 7 6 5 4 3

Distributed by National Book Network
4501 Forbes Blvd., Suite 200
Lanham, MD 20706
Phone: (800) 462-6420 Fax: (800) 338-4550
customercare@nbnbooks.com

ISBN: 978-1- 909487-17-8

Library of Congress Control Number:
2014946165

Daniel Green is hereby identified as the author of this work in accordance with Section 77 of the Copyright, Designs and Patents Act 1988

Editor: Vicki Murrell
Americanizer: Lee Faber
Design: Nicky Collings
Photography: Clare Winfield
Food styling: Rosie Reynolds
Styling: Wei Tang
Nutritional analysis: Fiona Hunter
Production: Nic Jones and David Hearn

Color reproduction by ALTA London
Printed and bound in China by Toppan Leefung Printing Ltd

Important notes
All recipe analysis is per portion.

The information and advice contained in this book is intended as a general guide to dieting and healthy eating and is not specific to individuals or their particular circumstances. This book is not intended to replace treatment by a qualified practitioner. Neither the author nor the publishers can be held responsible for claims arising from the inappropriate use of any dietary regime. Do not attempt self-diagnosis or self-treatment for serious or long-term conditions without consulting a medical professional or qualified practitioner.

The recipes in the book are color-coded according to food-combining principles (see page 20). Red recipes are made with acid-forming proteins, while green recipes are based around alkali-forming fruits and vegetables. Keeping these distinct avoids creating a pH imbalance in the stomach and assists with a healthy digestive process.

CONTENTS

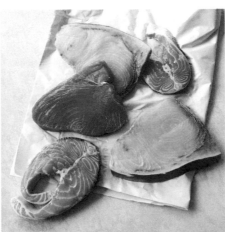

WHY I LOVE PALEO

My main priority has always been great-tasting food that is simple and healthy. When I create recipes, I want them to be ones that you will love and share with family and friends and that, as an added bonus, will help you lose weight and feel happy and healthier.

I know a lot about diets. As an overweight young adult, I lost 64 lb (29kg) and, in the 20 years since then, I have never put the weight back on. I have managed this by cutting out all junk and processed foods, and eating fresh fruit, vegetables, fish, meat, seeds, and nuts — essentially following the Paleo diet, even before the name and concept were well-known. It made sense to me. There is no need to see it as limiting or restrictive, as there is so much you *can* eat. That is what I embraced: delicious, fresh, healthy food that nourishes your body, and doesn't sacrifice taste or flavor — and, in fact, doesn't feel like a sacrifice at all.

PEOPLE WHO FOLLOW THE PALEO DIET REPORT A RANGE OF HEALTH BENEFITS:

- Increased energy levels
- Improved sleep
- Clearer skin and healthier looking hair
- Mental clarity
- Improved mood and attitude
- Less bloating and fewer digestive problems
- Fewer headaches and migraines
- Less joint and muscle pain
- Fewer colds and infections

WHAT IS
THE PALEO DIET?

Put simply, the Paleo diet is based on the foods your body was designed to eat:

MEAT FISH NUTS SEEDS FRUIT VEGETABLES

The way we eat now is wrong. We have become dependent on synthetic and heavily processed foods that are leading to serious health problems (diabetes and obesity), and even when we think we're being healthy, we're often eating food groups, such as grains, dairy, and legumes, which cause digestive distress, and result in chronic symptoms like sluggish energy levels, joint swelling, acid reflux, acne... the list just goes on and on.

There is a better way to eat and to live, and that is through the Paleo plan. Also referred to as the Caveman or Stone Age diet, "Paleo" refers to the Paleolithic Age, about 2.5 million years ago, when our hunter-gatherer ancestors ate a diet based on meat, fish, nuts, seeds, fruits, and vegetables — and thrived.

As our species has evolved, our lifestyle and the foods that we eat have changed dramatically. The Agrarian Revolution introduced grains, dairy, legumes, salt, sugar, and alcohol into our diet, and over the last century, with the use of agrochemicals in farming, the upward trend in processed convenience foods, and the use of chemicals as food additives, many believe that our diet has been subjected to more change than at any time over the previous three millennia.

Much of the food that we eat these days has been stripped of its nutrients and pumped full of bad fats, hidden salt, sugar, and a plethora of E numbers, such as colors, preservatives, humectants, emulsifiers, artificial flavors, acidity regulators and bulking agents. In fact, it's estimated that adults in the US eat an average of 11 lb of additives in just one year and research study after research study points to our declining health. Since 2000, the number of people in the US with both types of diabetes has increased from 17.5 million to 32.3 million in 2010, and by 2025 it is estimated that this number will have risen to over 50 million. Cardiovascular disease (CVD) causes almost 1 million deaths each year in the US, and a shocking 69% of adults over the age of 20 are overweight, which includes an estimated 36% who are obese (2010).

More and more people are developing hypersensitivities to gluten and lactose and, as this frequently remains undiagnosed, many people live with low-level, chronic symptoms of ill health for years.

It is therefore not surprising that a growing body of evidence is pointing to our modern eating habits as the root cause of many of the chronic diseases common today in the Western world. Our diet bears almost no relation to that of our Paleolithic ancestors and yet our human genetic make-up has changed relatively little since those times.

Many experts believe that the human body has not evolved genetically to deal with this modern way of eating, and that the natural diet of our Paleolithic ancestors could be the key to reducing our risk of many diseases and chronic ill health. However, better long-term health is only part of the story, as following the principles of the Paleo diet can bring enhanced energy levels, a healthier immune system, and a genuine feeling of well-being and vitality.

10 REASONS
TO EAT THE PALEO WAY

1
It's based on unprocessed, whole foods — which means fewer additives, unhealthy trans fats, and no hidden sugars or salt.

2
It's low in salt and rich in potassium — which means lower blood pressure.

3
It's high in fruit and vegetables — which means getting your 5 a day is simple.

4
It's low in saturated fat and high in healthy fats — which means lower cholesterol and less inflammation.

5
It's rich in protein and fiber — which means it helps you feel fuller for longer, and keeps hunger pangs at bay.

6
It helps to recalibrate your metabolism — which will help to shed any unwanted weight.

7
It's gluten-free — which helps to banish bloating and digestive problems.

8
It's low GI — which helps to avoid unhealthy spikes in blood sugar.

9
It's rich in plant-based phytochemicals — which can help reduce the risk of certain types of cancer, and conditions like dementia.

10
It helps balance the pH in your body — modern diets encourage the production of acid within the body, which is believed to increase calcium loss from the bone, and lead to many other health problems, including kidney stones, arthritis, fatigue, headaches, PMS, and skin disorders. In contrast, the Paleo diet helps create a more alkaline environment.

THE PALEO PRINCIPLES

Gastroenterologist Walter L. Voegtlin was one of the first scientists to suggest, in 1975, that following a Paleolithic-style diet could be the key to better health. Since then, there has been a growing body of evidence to support this idea, and one of the leading authorities on the diet, Professor Loren Cordain, a Professor at Colorado State University, has published several studies showing the benefits associated with the diet in renowned scientific journals including *The American Journal of Clinical Nutrition,* and *The British Journal of Nutrition.*

The core principles of Paleo are that the diet of our Paleolithic ancestors provides the blueprint for what and how we should eat today: eschewing grains, dairy, legumes, and vegetable oils, and eating high-quality meat, fish, eggs, fruit, vegetables, nuts, and seeds that provide us with all the nutrition that we need to lead an active, healthy life.

As you read on, you will see that foods are divided into those to "avoid," those to eat "in moderation," and those you are free to eat and enjoy as often as you like. The diet is still evolving, and there are a few gray areas regarding what our ancestors did in fact eat in Paleolithic times, and so the important thing to remember is that Paleo is not an all-or-nothing plan. The best approach is for you to become attuned to your body and find out what makes you feel happy, healthy, and energized. Be mindful of the main Paleo principles, but use them as a basis to create what is right for you.

The Paleo diet is a way of life. It isn't a plan that you follow for a period of time until you achieve a weight-loss goal, and then return to your old ways. However, once you've experienced the increased energy levels, and feeling of well-being that it offers, I guarantee you won't be tempted back by old bad habits. If you're still not convinced, why not give it a try for 2 weeks and see how you feel.

IN MODERATION

SALT

WHY? A high-salt diet will increase the risk of high blood pressure and upset the acid/alkali balance within the body, so use it only in moderation. I have specifically designed the recipes in this book without salt, and have used other flavors, such as herbs and spices, so that you won't miss it. It is very easy to acquire a "taste for salt," but it's also simple to lose this by gradually reducing the amount you add to food, and waiting for your taste buds to adapt.

RAW HONEY

WHY? The body processes all forms of sugar in the same way (even honey produces an insulin response in the body), so I recommend you only use raw honey or stevia (in moderation) as sweeteners. Raw honey is honey in its purest, most unprocessed form (it has not been heated or strained and still contains many of the nutrients that the bees put into it). Stevia is a natural, plant-sourced, caloric-free sugar substitute. (For best results, cut out all refined and added sugar for the first 30 days on the diet — you'll find that your taste buds adapt, and you enjoy the natural flavor of food without the need to add too much sweetness.)

ALCOHOL

WHY? The occasional glass of wine isn't a problem, and yet it is important to remember that alcohol is a toxin so "in moderation" is key. You should also avoid alcohol that is made from foods on the "avoid" list, such as beer (made from grain), vodka (made from potatoes), whiskey (made from grain) and sake (made from rice).

ROOT VEGETABLES

WHY? The issue of starchy vegetables is one of Paleo's gray areas. Potatoes are definitely on the "avoid" list, but other root vegetables, like sweet potatoes, don't contain the same antinutrients, and don't have such an adverse effect on blood sugar levels. Many hunter-gatherer groups, such as the Kitavans of Papua New Guinea, regularly eat yams, sweet potatoes, taro, and cassava (tapioca), and don't suffer any adverse effects. For this reason I include them here in the "in moderation" group.

VINEGAR

WHY? Strictly speaking, vinegar wasn't introduced to the human diet until after the Agricultural Revolution, so it wasn't around in the Paleolithic times — if you do want to use vinegar in moderation, choose apple cider vinegar, balsamic, or red/white wine vinegar rather than barley malt vinegar. Vinegar can upset the acid/alkali balance within the body, so use it only in moderation.

AVOID

PROCESSED FOODS

E.g., ready-made meals, fast food

WHY? You don't need a degree in nutrition to know that these foods are bad news, even for those not following a Paleo plan — pumped full of E numbers, salt and sugar, the problem is not just with what has been added, but what has been removed. Processed foods are often stripped of the very nutrients — dietary fiber, vitamins, minerals, and phytochemicals — that are good for you.

REFINED AND ADDED SUGARS

E.g., sugar, fructose, high-fructose corn syrup, corn sugar, corn syrup, agave syrup, golden syrup, malt syrup, molasses, rice syrup, jam, marmalade, jelly, ketchup, hoisin sauce, BBQ sauce, or anything with "dext" or "ose" in it

WHY? Unlike natural sugars (i.e., those you find in fruit, which come packaged with other nutrients), refined sugar provides nothing beneficial. All types of sugar (even unrefined natural sugars like honey) encourage the production of insulin, which leads to the laying down of fat.

GRAINS AND FOODS CONTAINING GRAINS

E.g., flour, barley, rice, corn, sorghum, amaranth, wild rice, buckwheat, spelt, rye, quinoa, bread, pasta, cookies, biscuits, crackers, cakes, bagels, muffins, pancakes, tortillas, couscous, oats, cereal, beer

WHY? Grains weren't introduced into our diet until after the Agrarian Revolution, so they weren't eaten by our Paleolithic ancestors. Gluten, a protein found in grains, such as wheat, rye, and barley, can irritate and damage the lining of the small intestine. This can lead to digestive problems, and interfere with the absorption of nutrients from food. Furthermore, in a processed form, grains have a high GI, which means they encourage the release of insulin, which in turn triggers fat storage. They also contain phytic acid, an antinutrient that can block the absorption of important minerals.

DAIRY AND FOODS CONTAINING DAIRY	E.g., milk, butter, cheese, crème fraîche, cream, ice cream, yogurt WHY? Cow's milk is designed to help calves grow quickly, not for humans to consume throughout their lives, and many believe we lack the digestive enzymes suited to this task. In fact, humans are the only species to continue drinking milk past weaning, and adults in most parts of the world do not consume many dairy products. Some estimates suggest that as much as three-quarters of the world is lactose-intolerant, to varying degrees, with symptoms including gas, bloating, cramps, indigestion, nausea, diarrhea, and constipation. Milk and dairy products are also considered to be acid-producing foods, which upset the acid–alkali balance in the body.
BEANS & LEGUMES	E.g., adzuki beans, baked beans, bean sprouts, black beans, black-eyed peas, cannellini beans, chickpeas, kidney beans, lentils, lima beans, snow peas, mung beans, peas, peanuts, peanut butter, pinto beans, sugar snap peas, soy, and related products (tofu, miso, soy milk, and soy sauce) WHY? Like cereals, beans and legumes contain antinutrients — lectins and phytic acid — which can irritate and damage the lining of the gut, and cause problems such as bloating and diarrhea. The damage caused by lectins is also thought to create a "leaky gut", meaning that other large particles can cross the intestinal barrier and enter your bloodstream. This is how food sensitivities start.
VEGETABLE AND SEED OILS	E.g., canola oil, palm oil, peanut oil, safflower oil, sunflower oil, soybean oil, margarine WHY? These oils are high in omega-6 fatty acids (very different from heart-healthy omega-3s) and promote inflammation — one of the major causes of heart disease, and other conditions such as arthritis.
POTATOES	WHY? Potatoes contain saponins — antinutrients that can damage the intestine. Also, because of the type of starch they contain, and the way they are prepared, they often have a high GI, which means they cause a spike in blood sugar levels that triggers the release of insulin.

GETTING STARTED

When you first start on the Paleo diet it can seem a little daunting, but with some careful preparation and planning, your new lifestyle will become second nature.

Experts recommend that, for the first 30 days, you stick to the diet rigidly in order to rid yourself of toxins and reset your body's biochemistry. This will also help you to make a clean break with bad habits. If your old way of eating consisted of heavily processed/junk foods, or lots of refined carbs or sugar, the first few days on Paleo could be tough. However, even if you believed your old style of eating was healthy and balanced, you might still find Paleo a challenge at the beginning, because of the sugar, salt and additives that are "hidden" in many foods that claim to be natural and healthy. Many people start to feel the benefits of the Paleo diet within the first few days, but for others, it can take a little longer. However, if you stick with it, you will start to feel and see the benefits, and once that happens, there's no looking back.

THE PALEO KITCHEN

A key part of the preparation for the Paleo diet is transforming your kitchen into a Paleo-friendly place. Clear all the forbidden foods from your fridge, freezer, shelves, and cupboards, and re-stock with all the foods from the list on pages 16–17.

I also recommend that you prepare your own food as much as you can, as then you will know exactly what is in it. When eating out, always inquire how the dish is made if you have any doubts. Also, when shopping, always read the food label, and be on your guard for any ingredients you don't recognize, with names that are hard to pronounce. Instead, look out for these guarantees of health and quality:

WATCH WORDS

· Organic, locally grown, seasonal produce — organic fruit and vegetables, grown without chemicals, are not just better for the environment, they are better for your body, because they are more nutritious.

· Grass-fed, free-range — meat reared this way has a better fatty acid balance (i.e., more omega-3 fats, fewer omega-6 fats). Eat meat that is free from antibiotic and other residues.

· Free-range — chickens grubbing in a field are far healthier than ones kept in cages, and studies have shown their eggs are nutritionally superior.

· Sustainably sourced — buy fish and shellfish from responsible sources for environmental reasons, preferably wild-caught, rather than farm-raised fish, as the latter are often fed chemicals and antibiotics, and have lower levels of protein and omega-3s.

THE 80/20 RULE

If the idea of never having a bagel, a bowl of muesli, or a glass of wine ever again fills you with terror, don't worry. The Paleo diet has an 80/20 rule, which means that, providing you stick to the rules 80% of the time, you don't need to be quite so strict for the other 20%. You can lapse a little, and treat yourself to the odd slice of toast or sugary dessert. However, I recommend that you start by following the diet to the letter for at least a few weeks, just to see how much better you feel. And, with this book of fantastic recipes, you'll struggle to find a reason to cook anything else!

A 10-DAY PALEO TRIAL

IN ONE STUDY, PUBLISHED IN THE *EUROPEAN JOURNAL OF CLINICAL NUTRITION*, SCIENTISTS FROM THE UNIVERSITY OF CALIFORNIA FOUND THAT, AFTER JUST 10 DAYS OF EATING A PALEO DIET, VOLUNTEERS HAD IMPROVED BLOOD SUGAR CONTROL, INCREASED SENSITIVITY TO INSULIN, REDUCED BLOOD PRESSURE, AND REDUCED LEVELS OF TOTAL CHOLESTEROL, LDL OR "BAD" CHOLESTEROL, AND TRIGLYCERIDES IN THEIR BLOOD.

WHAT TO BUY

MEAT, FISH & EGGS

fresh meat, poultry, game and offal — beef, chicken, duck, game birds, goat, lamb, pork, rabbit, turkey, veal, venison, wild boar

eggs — hen's, quail's, or duck's, even emu's

fish (and fish eggs) and shellfish (canned and fresh)

FRUIT & VEG

apples, apricots, bananas, berries, cherries, citrus fruits, cranberries, dates, dragon fruit, figs, grapes, kiwis, lychees, mangos, melons, nectarines, passion fruit, peaches, pears, persimmons, pineapples, plums, pomegranates, star fruit

artichokes, asparagus, butternut squash, Brussels sprouts, bok choy, broccoli, cabbages, carrots, cauliflower, celery, cucumbers, eggplant, kale, kohlrabi, leeks, lettuces, marrows, mushrooms, okra, olives, onions, parsnips, pumpkins, radishes, spinach, watercress, tomatoes, turnips, zucchini

sea vegetables — kombu, nori, wakame, other seaweeds and algaes

canned fruit and vegetables (but make sure they are sugar- and sodium-free)

NUTS

almonds, Brazil nuts, cashews, chestnuts, hazelnuts, macadamias, pecans, pine nuts, pistachios, walnuts (Note: peanuts are not Paleo-friendly because they are legumes, not nuts)

nut butters — almond, cashew, macadamia

almond flour — blanched almonds, ground up into a fine powder — a great ingredient for baking, and can be used in place of regular wheat flour

SEEDS

flaxseed, pumpkin seeds, sesame seeds, sunflower seeds

OILS & FATS

avocado oil, coconut oil, flaxseed oil, hazelnut oil, macadamia nut oil, olive oil, sesame oil, walnut oil

lard, tallow

DRINKS

filtered or spring water, herbal tea, coconut water, freshly juiced fruit and vegetables

FLAVORINGS & SAUCES

fish sauce — many fish sauces are not Paleo as they have added fructose and sugar, or hydrolyzed wheat protein. However, the Red Boat brand is a rare exception — it's only made from two ingredients (freshly caught wild black anchovies and sea salt) and is minimally processed.

curry paste — many curry pastes are Paleo, just make sure you read the label to check the ingredients. It's also very easy to make yourself.

sea salt — produced through evaporation of ocean water or lake seawater, and so undergoes little processing. Table salt is usually mined and contains additives, which is why sea salt is better.

coconut aminos — a soy-free seasoning sauce made from coconut tree sap; this is a great substitute for soy sauce

mustard — make sure it is gluten- and dairy-free

tomato paste and sun-dried tomato paste — make sure it is gluten-free with no added sugar or salt

meat, fish, and vegetable bouillon — organic and low-salt are the best options, or it's very simple to make your own

arrowroot — a natural thickener that can be used in place of cornstarch or wheat flour to thicken sauces

herbs and spices — add great flavor to food, and are a source of many vitamins, minerals, and phytochemicals

SWEETENERS

raw honey — add in place of sugar when you want sweetness. Raw honey is often solid, and you just need to warm it up a little to get it to a liquid state.

stevia — a plant that has been used as a sweetener for centuries in Paraguay and Brazil (now commonly available as naturally sourced sugar substitute)

COCONUT

coconut flour — natural, dried coconut that is ground into a fine powder. Also a great substitute for wheat flour.

coconut milk — a great substitute for milk and makes the most delicious curries. Look for brands that don't contain guar gum or preservatives, and always go for the "light" version to keep the fat content low.

shredded, unsweetened coconut

FAQ

IS THE DIET SUITABLE FOR CHILDREN?

The Paleo diet is a nutrient-dense diet and can provide all the nutrition that a growing child needs. In fact, some people would argue that, because it cuts out heavily processed/refined foods and things like sweets and cookies, the Paleo diet is better for children than a traditional Western diet. Having said that, however, it's important to remember that children are still developing and growing, and as a result, they have needs, particularly for nutrients like calcium, which should be taken very seriously. In practical terms, it is important to plan their diet carefully to ensure that it provides enough energy (calories) and other nutrients to support their growth. While low-carb diets are fine and dandy for fully grown adults, carbs are a useful source of energy for a growing child, so many parents relax the rules slightly, and add in a few unprocessed carbs like potatoes, sweet potatoes, and other starchy vegetables.

IS THE DIET SUITABLE FOR PEOPLE WITH DIABETES?

One of the benefits of the Paleo plan is improved insulin sensitivity, and better blood sugar control — two big plus points for people with type 2 diabetes. Furthermore, diabetics have a greater risk of heart disease, so the fact that the diet is low in salt, and rich in healthy fats is another bonus. However, while there is no restriction on the amount of fruit eaten on the diet, it does contain natural sugars, so diabetics need to watch the amount they consume carefully. People with insulin-dependent (type 1) diabetes should discuss the diet with their dietician or doctor before giving it a try.

IS THE PALEO DIET SUITABLE FOR VEGETARIANS?

Meat and fish were an integral part of the diet of Paleolithic Man, and they are a major source of protein in the Paleo diet. Grains and legumes, an important source of protein in many vegetarian diets, are not allowed on the Paleo diet, and so the truth is that it can be difficult to follow as a vegetarian. I recommend vegetarians consult a dietician to discuss adapting the diet to their needs before giving it a try.

I'M PREGNANT. CAN I FOLLOW THE PALEO PLAN?

Yes, the Paleo diet is perfectly capable of providing all the nutrients a pregnant woman needs, and can even help reduce the risk of some pregnancy-related conditions, such as gestational diabetes.

WILL THE DIET HELP ME LOSE WEIGHT?

Although Paleo is not designed as a weight-loss diet, many people find that it helps them shed unwanted weight. There are several explanations for this: cutting out highly refined/high GI carbs reduces the amount of insulin that the body needs to produce, and as insulin encourages the body to lay down fat, the reduction in insulin makes it easier to lose weight. Another theory is that it helps to recalibrate your metabolism, so that you burn more calories. The fact that the diet is high in protein and fiber will also help, because these nutrients help you feel full quicker, and for longer, so you're less likely to overeat.

HOW CAN I MAKE SURE I GET ENOUGH CALCIUM ON THE DIET?

Dairy products are rich in calcium, which is important for strong, healthy bones. However, there are plenty of other non-dairy, Paleo-friendly sources:

· fish that is eaten with bones, such as sardines or canned salmon

· kale and other leafy green vegetables

· nuts and seeds, particularly almonds and sesame seeds

· dried apricots and figs

· oranges

	RDA calcium		Calcium (mg)
Children 4–6 years	450mg	3½ oz sardines	500mg
Children 7–10 years	550mg	3 oz steamed kale	120mg
Boys 11–18 years	1000mg	1 oz almonds	60mg
Girls 11–18 years	800mg	2 tbsp almond butter	86mg
Men and women	700mg	3½ oz canned salmon	300mg
Breast-feeding women	1250mg	1oz dried apricots	25mg
Women after menopause	1000mg	1 tbsp sesame seeds	100mg
		1 orange	70mg
		3 oz steamed broccoli	32mg
		3½ oz watercress	170mg

HOW TO
USE THIS BOOK

The Paleo recipes in this book are guaranteed to bring you many health benefits, and weight loss is often simply an additional bonus. However, if you have bought this book with a specific weight-loss goal in mind, I have designed it in a way that I believe will maximize your efforts, and that I hope you will find beneficial.

As I have said, as a teenager I piled on the pounds. I realized that, in order to lose weight, I needed to change the way that I thought about food, and so I set about researching the best, most effective way to go about this. I became very interested in the work of the New York physician, William Howard Hay, who was the first to develop the concept of "food combining" and whose theories have proved extremely influential in the world of modern dieting.

Hay's research gave him the idea that certain foods require an acid pH environment for digestion, whereas other foods require the opposite, an alkaline environment. As most meals contain a mix of the two, the digestion of both cannot take place at the same time and the result is often a chemical imbalance that leads to many symptoms of digestive distress. Hay's solution to this problem

was to create meals from alkali-forming foods (such as fruits and vegetables) and from acid-forming foods (concentrated proteins such as meat, game, fish, cheese, and eggs) and never to combine the two. Concentrated carbohydrates, or starch foods (grains, bread, all foods containing flour, all sugars, and foods containing sucrose, but not the naturally occurring sugars found in fruit) were then grouped into another acid-forming category, but these again were to be kept separate from proteins, as they, too needed different conditions for digestion.

In order to lose weight, I incorporated Hay's approach into my eating habits and have never looked back. As it worked for me I believe it can work for you too, and so in this book you will find that the recipes are color coded.

The green recipes are dishes that are based around alkali-forming fruits and vegetables, while the red recipes feature acid-forming proteins. To ensure a balanced diet, and the best weight-loss results, I recommend that you choose red recipes for an entire day, and then switch to green recipes the next day, and alternate throughout the week. However, you could also start with a red breakfast, and then have a green lunch and go back to red for dinner — whichever you prefer. And, of course, if you simply want to follow the Paleo plan, just ignore the color-coding and go with any recipe that takes your fancy. Whatever your preferred approach, I promise you excellent results.

So get cooking! Start following these recipes today, and join the Paleo revolution!

BREAKFASTS
& BRUNCHES

You'll be served these little steamed egg soups for breakfast in most hotels in Asia, and they're also popular as an appetizer. Their texture should be smooth and bubble-free, and the key is to simmer them on as low a heat as possible, for as long as possible.

JAPANESE SAVORY CUSTARD (CHAWANMUSHI)

153 calories | 10.3g fat | 2.7g saturates | 0.3g sugar | 0.9g salt | 15.5g protein | 0.2g fiber

Serves 4

6 eggs
vegetable stock or dashi
  – volume to equal that
  of the eggs
1 teaspoon Paleo-
  friendly fish sauce,
  such as Red Boat (not
  necessary if using
  dashi)
8 large cooked shrimp
4 straw or shiitake
  mushrooms, very
  thinly sliced
1 scallion, cut into
  matchsticks

Crack the eggs into a medium-sized bowl and, using chopsticks, lightly whisk until blended, without incorporating too much air. Stir in the dashi or stock and add the fish sauce, if using.

Divide the mixture between 4 small serving bowls, each about the size of a ramekin.

Cover these bowls or wrap them in plastic wrap, and steam over low heat (the water should be at a gentle simmer) for 15–20 minutes, or until the eggs are set — a bamboo steamer is great for this.

Immediately transfer the bowls to the refrigerator to chill for at least 3 hours or overnight.

Unwrap the custards. Top with the shrimp, mushrooms and scallions, and serve.

TIP DASHI IS A TRADITIONAL JAPANESE BROTH MADE FROM BONITO FLAKES AND KOMBU (KELP — HIGH IN POTASSIUM, CALCIUM, AND IODINE AS WELL AS VITAMINS A AND C). IT OFTEN HAS RICE WINE OR VINEGAR, AND SOY SAUCE ADDED FOR FLAVOR, BUT YOU CAN REPLACE THESE WITH PALEO-FRIENDLY COCONUT WATER VINEGAR (SOMETIMES JUST CALLED COCONUT VINEGAR) AND COCONUT AMINOS (MADE FROM RAW COCONUT TREE SAP AND SUN-DRIED SEA SALT — IT TASTES JUST LIKE SOY SAUCE).

Pancakes always make a delicious weekend brunch — and who says you can't have them on a Paleo diet? Simply replace regular flour with coconut and almond flour and you can achieve light, fluffy, gluten-free results.

PANCAKES WITH
BERRIES AND MAPLE SYRUP

532 calories | 37.6g fat | 5.7g saturates | 18.5g sugar | 0.4g salt | 24.5g protein | 12g fiber

Serves 2

1 cup almond flour
1 tablespoon coconut
    flour
3 eggs
¼ cup water
⅓ cup prune juice
¼ teaspoon freshly
    grated nutmeg
olive oil spray
1½ cups fresh berries
1 tablespoon grade B
    maple syrup, or melted
    raw honey

In a large mixing bowl, whisk the flours, eggs, and water together until you have a smooth batter. Any lumps should soon disappear with a little mixing. Whisk in the prune juice and nutmeg, and set aside for a minute or two.

Place a nonstick frying pan over medium heat, and allow to get hot — about 2–3 minutes. Spray the pan with a little oil, and add a spoonful of batter (it is best not to crowd the pan, so make these pancakes one at a time). Let the batter bubble a little, and cook for a minute, then flip and cook for 1–2 minutes on the reverse side.

Turn onto a plate, and serve with fresh berries, and a drizzle of maple syrup or honey.

TIP WHEN YOU MAKE THESE PANCAKES, TRY AND COOK THEM AS SOON AS THE BATTER IS MADE, AS THE COCONUT FLOUR CAN SWELL AND THICKEN OVER TIME — IT DOESN'T KEEP OVERNIGHT.

TIP THE PALEO PLAN CUTS OUT ALL PROCESSED, REFINED SUGARS, BUT DOES ALLOW A FEW NATURAL SWEETENERS. THE BEST TYPES TO USE ARE GRADE B MAPLE SYRUP, WHICH IS 100% PURE AND DISTILLED NATURALLY, AND RAW HONEY, WHICH IS AGAIN UNPROCESSED, AND CONTAINS ALL THE NUTRIENTS THE BEES PUT INTO IT.

Everyone loves sushi, but rice is not allowed on the Paleo plan, so these rolls are the next best thing. I first made them for a boutique hotel in Bangkok called VIE, and they are still on the menu, though I change the fillings every now and then.

NO-RICE
BREAKFAST SUSHI

406 calories | 27.5g fat | 5.9g saturates | 0g sugar | 4.5g salt | 41g protein | 0.6g fiber

Serves 2

4 eggs
freshly ground black
  pepper
½ tablespoon olive oil
2 large sheets of seaweed
  paper (nori)
2 tablespoons chopped
  chives
8 oz smoked salmon

Crack two of the eggs into a bowl, and beat with a fork until smooth. Season with freshly ground black pepper.

Heat a heavy nonstick frying pan over high heat and add the oil. When hot, tip the eggs into the pan. Swirl to coat the base thoroughly, and allow the eggs to set slightly. Cook for 1–2 minutes. Remove from the heat, tip the omelet onto a plate (do not fold) and repeat the process with the two remaining eggs.

Lay a sheet of the seaweed paper out flat on a clean kitchen surface, and place one of the omelets on top. Scatter with chives, and layer half the smoked salmon on top. Season to taste.

Fold the bottom edge of the seaweed over the filling, then roll it up firmly. Dampen the top border with a little water to help it seal. Repeat with the second omelet and sheet of seaweed paper.

Using a serrated knife, cut off the ends to neaten them, and slice each roll into 4–6 rounds. Serve immediately.

VARIATION BACON IS ALSO A VERY TASTY ADDITION TO A BREAKFAST SUSHI ROLL. HOWEVER, ENSURE THAT YOU BUY THE BEST-QUALITY MEAT YOU CAN FIND — IT WON'T BE AS HEAVILY PROCESSED AS THE MASS-PRODUCED, CHEAPER VARIETIES.

Soufflés often get people a little scared. However, they're as easy as anything, so please don't be intimidated. They do deflate a little when you take them out of the oven, but don't panic if this happens — it doesn't mean it's a disaster!

EGG SOUFFLÉ

OMELET

314 calories | 19.5g fat | 5g saturates | 2g sugar | 2.4g salt | 34.1g protein | 0.8g fiber

Serves 1

2 eggs, plus 2 egg whites
1 teaspoon olive oil
6 cherry tomatoes,
  halved
2½ oz ham (very
  good quality, not
  pre-sliced), chopped
freshly ground black
  pepper
1 tablespoon chopped
  chives

Preheat the broiler to high.

Crack the eggs, separating the yolks from the whites in separate bowls. Add the two extra egg whites.

Whisk the whites vigorously for about a minute until light and fluffy, then whisk the yolks, and add them to the whites. Fold in carefully.

Heat the oil in a wide, nonstick frying pan with a heatproof handle, and add the egg mix, swirling the pan so it coats the bottom. Leave to cook for a couple of minutes, then add the tomatoes and ham and season with black pepper.

Transfer the pan to the broiler, and leave for a few minutes until the eggs are puffed up, soufflé-like, and golden.

Remove from the heat and slide onto a plate. Scatter the chives on top, and serve immediately.

TIP EGGS MAKE THE PERFECT BREAKFAST IF YOU'RE TRYING TO LOSE WEIGHT, AS THE PROTEIN AND FAT HELP SUSTAIN YOUR ENERGY LEVELS, ARMING YOU AGAINST THOSE CRAVINGS FOR A MID-MORNING SNACK.

Sun-dried tomatoes are a great ingredient to have stocked in your Paleo-friendly kitchen, as they have a rich flavor, and an almost meaty texture, so guarantee a very satisfying start to the day — especially nice for a weekend brunch.

OMELET WITH
SUN-DRIED TOMATOES

350 calories | 27g fat | 6.3g saturates | 3.8g sugar | 0.9g salt | 24.4g protein | 1.7g fiber

Serves 4

12 eggs
freshly ground black
    pepper
1 tablespoon olive oil
1½ red onions, thinly
    sliced
2 tablespoons chopped
    sun-dried tomatoes
12 cherry tomatoes,
    halved
a handful of basil leaves,
    shredded, plus extra
    to serve
1½ cups chopped
    watercress

It's best to cook one omelet at a time, so start by breaking three eggs into a large mixing bowl and beating them lightly with a fork. Season with a little black pepper.

Turn the broiler on to its highest setting.

Heat a drizzle of olive oil in a large, nonstick frying pan, and fry the onion until soft and slightly caramelized. Transfer the onion to a plate and set aside.

Add the beaten egg to the frying pan, swirling the pan to cover the base as it sets.

Scatter a quarter of the cooked onions, sun-dried tomatoes, cherry tomatoes, and basil over the top of the omelet and slide the pan under the hot broiler for 1–2 minutes, or until golden.

Slide the omelet onto a plate and keep warm while you cook the remaining omelets. Serve with some fresh, peppery watercress, and a little extra basil.

If you feel hungry and need a larger portion, add more egg whites to the pan. Egg whites have all the protein, which helps you stay fuller for longer, without the fat of the yolk.

SCRAMBLED EGGS
WITH AVOCADO SALSA

450 calories | 38.2g fat | 9.4g saturates | 3.5g sugar | 0.7g salt | 24.5g protein | 4.6g fiber

Serves 2

1 ripe Hass avocado, chopped
a handful of basil leaves, torn
1 large tomato, seeded and chopped
2 scallions, finely chopped
6 eggs
freshly ground black pepper
½ tablespoon olive oil

Place the avocado, basil, tomato, and scallions in a bowl, and mix together.

In a separate bowl, lightly whisk the eggs, and season with a few grinds of black pepper.

Heat the olive oil in a nonstick saucepan over medium heat. Add the eggs to the pan and let the mixture rest for about half a minute, then stir with a wooden spoon, lifting and folding and turning until they are lightly set, and slightly runny in places.

Remove from the heat and leave the eggs for a few seconds to continue cooking.

Divide the eggs between two plates, and spoon the avocado salsa alongside.

TIP YOU CAN REDUCE THE AMOUNT OF AVOCADO, AND UP THE QUANTITY OF TOMATO TO LOWER THE FAT CONTENT, BUT DON'T FORGET THAT AVOCADO IS A SOURCE OF HEALTHY, MONOUNSATURATED FAT THAT IS QUICKLY BURNED FOR ENERGY.

This healthy breakfast is perfect all-around. The salmon is an excellent source of omega-3 fatty acids — essential for brain function, warding off heart disease, and maintaining healthy hair and nails — while poaching eggs is the best way to cook them without adding any extra fat into the equation.

POACHED EGGS
WITH SMOKED SALMON

310 calories | 19.8g fat | 5.1g saturates | 0.4g sugar | 3.9g salt | 33.1g protein | 0g fiber

Serves 4

⅔ cup white vinegar
1 lb smoked salmon
4 eggs
2 tablespoons chopped
  chives
freshly ground black
  pepper

Fill a saucepan just over half full with cold water, and bring it to a boil. Add the vinegar (the ratio should be about 4:1, water to vinegar).

Meanwhile, divide the smoked salmon between four serving plates. When the water is at a fast boil, crack one egg into one side of the pan and another egg into the other side. (I recommend doing no more than two at a time, or the pan will boil over.) Cook the eggs for 3–4 minutes.

Remove the eggs with a slotted spoon, and place in a bowl of tepid water to keep warm while you cook the other eggs.

When all the eggs are poached, you can refresh the water in the bowl to completely remove the taste of vinegar.

When ready to serve, place an egg on each plate of salmon, scatter with fresh chives and season with a few grinds of black pepper.

TIP IT IS GOOD TO ADD VINEGAR TO THE WATER WHEN POACHING EGGS, AS IT HELPS THE WHITES TO FIRM UP FASTER. FRESH EGGS ARE EASIER TO POACH AS THEY HOLD THEIR SHAPE BETTER — THE WHITES GATHER AROUND THE YOLKS, RESULTING IN A ROUNDER, PERFECT, POACHED EGG SHAPE.

These cookies are a real treat, as very few baking ingredients are compatible with the Paleo diet. However, this recipe creates delicious, crumbly coconut cookies without using any butter — genius!

CRUMBLY COCONUT COOKIES

125 calories | 6.3g fat | 3.8g saturates | 3.7g sugar | 0.2g salt | 6.1g protein | 5.6g fiber

Makes 10-12 cookies

scant ½ cup light coconut milk
4 eggs, beaten
1⅓ cups coconut flour
1½ tablespoons raw honey

Preheat the oven to 400°F and line a baking sheet with parchment paper.

Put all the ingredients in a large bowl, and stir to mix well. As it becomes like a soft dough, use your hands to combine.

Spoon the mixture into 10–12 small rounds, about 1 inch in diameter, and place them, spaced evenly apart, on the baking sheet. Bake in the oven for 10–12 minutes, or until golden brown.

Remove from the oven, and allow to cool for a few minutes, then turn out onto a wire rack to cool completely before serving.

TIP THESE COOKIES CAN FALL APART IF YOU OVERCOOK THEM, SO ERR ON THE SIDE OF CAUTION, AND SLIGHTLY UNDERCOOK, LEAVING THEM TO COOK THROUGH WHILE THEY COOL.

I first tried this fantastic banana bread when filming a show with the American cooking icon, Paula Deen. I have tried many versions to reduce the fat, and think this one is the winner.

WALNUT AND BANANA BREAD

220 calories | 15.8g fat | 1.9g saturates | 11.3g sugar | 0.1g salt | 7.5g protein | 2.3g fiber

Serves 8

oil, for greasing
2 ripe bananas
3 eggs
1 heaping cup almond flour
1½ tablespoons raw honey
¾ cup walnuts, roughly chopped

Preheat the oven to 350°F and lightly oil an 8 x 4½ inch nonstick loaf pan.

In a large bowl, mash the bananas thoroughly with a fork. In a separate bowl, whisk together the eggs, then add the flour and honey. Stir in the walnuts and mashed banana.

Pour the cake mixture into the pan and bake for 20–30 minutes, or until a thin skewer inserted into the center of the cake comes out clean.

Remove from the oven and cool in the pan for a few minutes, then turn out onto a wire rack to cool completely before serving.

TIP WALNUTS ARE HIGH IN CALORIES AND FAT, BUT LIKE AVOCADOS, IT IS THE HEALTHY KIND OF FAT, WHICH KEEPS YOU FEELING FULL. THEY'RE ALSO A GREAT SOURCE OF FIBER AND PROTEIN.

Porridge (oatmeal) always hits the spot on a cold winter's morning, and this oat-free version means you don't have to go without on the Paleo plan. It is high in carbohydrates, but as long as you eat this in the morning, you can burn them off throughout the day.

OAT-FREE
PALEO PORRIDGE

454 calories | 31.5g fat | 11.5g saturates | 32g sugar | trace salt | 9g protein | 6.5g fiber

Serves 1

2 tablespoons shredded coconut

1 tablespoon almond flour

1 teaspoon pumpkin seeds

1 teaspoon ground cinnamon

2 tablespoons chopped walnuts, plus extra to serve

1 cup boiling water

1 tablespoon raw honey, melted

½ banana, sliced

Place all the ingredients except the water, honey and banana in a food processor and blend together to a fine powder.

Pour the boiling water over the mix and stir to combine.

Serve in a bowl with honey drizzled on top, a scattering of crushed nuts and freshly sliced banana.

TIP OATS ARE EXCLUDED ON THE PALEO PLAN AND FOR GOOD REASON — THEY'RE OFTEN CONTAMINATED WITH OTHER GLUTEN GRAINS DURING PROCESSING, PLUS THEY RESULT IN A HUGE SPIKE IN BLOOD SUGAR LEVELS.

This fruit cup sundae provides you with a great boost of breakfast energy. If you want to lower the carbohydrates, just swap the bananas for more berries and citrus fruits. You can make this the night before to have on the run.

FRUIT CUP SUNDAE

498 calories | 28.6g fat | 3.6g saturates | 47.7g sugar | 0g salt | 9g protein | 6.3g fiber

Serves 4

4 ripe bananas, peeled
10 oz mixed berries
   (strawberries,
   raspberries and
   blueberries are great)
½ cup unsalted walnuts
½ cup unsalted cashews
½ cup unsalted pecans
3 tablespoons raw honey,
   melted

In a bowl, mash the bananas with a fork and set aside. If using strawberries, cut them into ½-inch slices and set aside.

Place the nuts in a sealed plastic bag and bash with a rolling pin a few times to crush. Transfer to a bowl, add the honey and stir to mix well.

In individual glass bowls or cocktail glasses, layer the bananas, berries and nuts, repeating until you reach the top.

TIP RAW HONEY HAS ANTISEPTIC, ANTIBIOTIC, ANTIFUNGAL, AND ANTIBACTERIAL PROPERTIES, AND IT NEVER SPOILS! IT IS GENERALLY MORE SOLID THAN REGULAR HONEY, BUT IF YOU HEAT IT A LITTLE, IT WILL MELT, AND CAN BE DRIZZLED JUST LIKE LIQUID HONEY.

This is a vitamin-rich power breakfast smoothie — essential for those days when you wake up feeling sluggish. The apples cover the detox angle, while the kale, banana, and honey will provide you with energy to spare.

POWER BREAKFAST BLEND

183 calories | 6g fat | 4.9g saturates | 29.5g sugar | 0.1g salt | 2g protein | 4.3g fiber

Serves 2

1 apple, cored
1 ripe banana, peeled
a large handful
   of spinach or kale
1 tablespoon coconut
   oil

1 teaspoon vanilla
   extract
1 teaspoon ground
   cinnamon
1 teaspoon raw
   honey

Blend everything in a food processor or blender until smooth, and serve over ice.

Raw honey and grade B maple syrup are the natural sweeteners allowed on Paleo. You can use either in any of these recipes. The mint is a must though, as it lifts this smoothie with a burst of fresh flavor — lovely in the morning!

ENERGIZER

333 calories | 13.3g fat | 11.4g saturates | 44.2g sugar | trace salt | 4.8g protein | 3.7g fiber

Serves 2

2 ripe bananas, peeled
1 tablespoon raw honey
1½ cups strawberries
⅔ cup light coconut milk
a handful of ice
a few mint leaves, to
   serve

Place all the ingredients except the mint in a blender and whizz until smooth. Serve with a sprig of mint.

TIP THE PALEO DIET DOES NOT ENCOURAGE CAFFEINE. HOWEVER, IF YOU ARE FOLLOWING THE PLAN LONG-TERM, IT IS POSSIBLE YOU MIGHT INDULGE A LITTLE FROM TIME TO TIME. ADDING AN ESPRESSO SHOT TO THIS SMOOTHIE WILL PROVIDE YOU WITH AN EXTRA BOOST OF ENERGY, SO KEEP IT IN RESERVE FOR WHEN YOU NEED IT MOST.

This is such a delicious way to start the day. The mango has natural sugar and carbohydrates to get you going in the morning, while the coconut milk will keep you feeling full until lunch.

MANGO
BREAKFAST SMOOTHIE

252 calories | 14.2g fat | 11.4g saturates | 29g sugar | 0.3g salt | 2.6g protein | 8.2g fiber

Serves 2

2 ripe mangoes, peeled and pitted
1 heaping cup light coconut milk
½ teaspoon ground cinnamon

Place all the mango flesh, plus the coconut milk and cinnamon into a blender, and purée until smooth. Serve over ice.

TIP TRYING TO GET ALL THE FLESH OUT OF A MANGO CAN LEAVE YOU WITH A BIG, JUICY MESS. THE BEST WAY TO DO IT IS TO TAKE A SHARP KNIFE AND SLICE THE FRUIT VERTICALLY, AS CLOSE TO EITHER SIDE OF THE STONE AS POSSIBLE. NEXT, HOLD EACH MANGO SLICE FLESH-SIDE UP, AND SCORE THE FLESH IN A GRID PATTERN ALL THE WAY DOWN TO THE SKIN. NOW TURN THE SKIN INSIDE OUT AND CUT THE MANGO CUBES INTO A BOWL, ADDING ALL THE JUICES THAT ARE LEFT ON THE PLATE, AND THERE IS NO WASTE!

LIGHT MEALS, SNACKS & SIDES

This recipe contains all the good fats, plus lots of protein, so it will keep you feeling full and banish hunger cravings between meals. Quail's eggs might seem elegant and decadent, but they are not at all expensive. Look in your local Asian supermarkets to get the best prices.

SALMON, AVOCADO, AND QUAIL'S EGGS

504 calories | 41.7g fat | 9.3g saturates | 0.8g sugar | 2.5g salt | 30.2g protein | 3.4g fiber

Serves 4

12 quail's eggs
1 tablespoon white
    vinegar
3 tablespoons olive oil
1 teaspoon Dijon
    mustard
10³/₄ oz smoked salmon
2 avocados, thinly sliced
1 lemon, quartered
dill, to garnish

Fill a saucepan two-thirds full with water and bring to a boil. Add the quail's eggs (do not overcrowd the pan) and cook for 4–5 minutes, depending on your preference, then drain and allow to cool before peeling.

Make the dressing by whisking together the vinegar, oil, and mustard.

Slice the quail's eggs in half, and divide them between four plates, along with the salmon and avocado.

Drizzle the vinaigrette on top and serve with lemon wedges, and a scattering of fresh dill.

TIP TINY, SPECKLED QUAIL'S EGGS ARE INCREDIBLY PRETTY AND MAKE A VERY CLASSY ADDITION TO MANY SOUPS, SALADS AND APPETIZERS. THEY'RE ALSO LOW IN CALORIES, RICH IN PROTEIN, AND FULL OF ESSENTIAL NUTRIENTS, SUCH AS VITAMIN D AND B12, SELENIUM, AND CHOLINE.

I have worked a lot throughout Asia — mainly in Hong Kong, Thailand, and Malaysia — and I love to cook this style of food, as it's so full of delicious flavor and is easy to make at home. This is a perfect example. Add a little chili and Hoisin sauce if you are not following the Paleo plan so strictly.

PORK AND
BEEF CABBAGE ROLLS

213 calories | 9g fat | 3.6g saturates | 3.6g sugar | 0.1g salt | 26.8g protein | 1.9g fiber

Serves 4

15–20 cabbage leaves
7 oz lean ground beef
7 oz lean ground pork
1 onion, finely chopped
3 garlic cloves, crushed
2 bird's eye chilies,
  finely chopped
1 quart vegetable
  bouillon

Bring a large pan of water to a boil, and blanch the cabbage leaves for 1–2 minutes, then drain, refresh in ice water, and set aside.

In a bowl, mix the beef, pork, onion, garlic, and chili, stirring to incorporate well.

Lay a cabbage leaf on a clean surface, and place a large spoonful of the meat mixture in the center. Fold the sides of the leaf over to cover the filling, and then roll into a small parcel, pinning with a cocktail stick to seal. Repeat until you have used up all the filling.

In a large saucepan, bring the bouillon to a boil. Carefully lower the cabbage rolls into the pan, and simmer for 15 minutes, or until the meat filling is cooked through.

Serve the cabbage rolls in a bowl with a ladleful of the bouillon.

TIP DON'T FORGET TO REFRESH THE LEAVES IN ICE WATER AS THIS WILL ENSURE THE CABBAGE STOPS COOKING, AND STAYS A VIBRANT GREEN.

Serve this at a party, and I guarantee you'll impress your guests — the presentation is fantastic. To achieve a perfectly shaped tower, all you need is a pastry ring, but if you don't have one on hand, it's easy to make your own by taking the top and bottom off a tuna can.

SALMON AND
AVOCADO TOWER

397 calories | 31.7g fat | 5.9g saturates | 1.6g sugar | 0.2g salt | 25.2g protein | 3.8g fiber

Serves 4

2 x 7 oz skinless salmon fillets
juice of 1 lemon
2 tablespoons olive oil
4–6 chives, finely chopped, plus extra to garnish
2 ripe avocados, peeled, halved, and pitted
2 scallions, finely chopped
½ red onion, finely chopped
freshly ground black pepper
3 oz salmon roe

Using a sharp knife, chop the salmon into very small cubes (making sure you discard any bones you find). Transfer the salmon to a bowl, and pour over half the lemon juice.

Add in the olive oil and chives, and mix together well, then set aside.

Scoop the avocado flesh into a bowl, and mash with a fork. Squeeze over the remaining lemon juice so it does not discolor. Add the scallions and red onion, and mix in well with a few grinds of black pepper.

Place four small pastry rings on four individual plates and fill each a quarter full with a layer of avocado. Add a layer of cured salmon to almost reach the top of the mold, and then top with a layer of salmon roe. Finish with a garnish of chives and serve.

TIP YOU CAN ALSO USE TROUT ROE FOR THIS RECIPE, AS IT'S VERY TASTY, AND A LITTLE LESS EXPENSIVE THAN SALMON ROE.

I love tuna tartare, and have created and tasted many different versions over the years. However, this one, representing the flavors of Asia, has to be my favorite. Add a little green chili if you like things spicy.

ASIAN TUNA

TARTARE

322 calories | 20.7g fat | 4.2g saturates | 1.8g sugar | 0.2g salt | 31.3g protein | 2.6g fiber

Serves 4

2 x 9 oz tuna steaks (very fresh)
1 tablespoon sesame seeds, plus extra to garnish
2 tablespoons sesame oil
2 tablespoons lemon juice
½ red onion, finely chopped
4 scallions, chopped
1 avocado, finely cubed
a handful of fresh cilantro, plus extra to garnish

Finely chop the tuna steaks and then place in a large bowl with the sesame seeds, sesame oil, lemon juice, red onion, scallion, and avocado. Mix well. Add the cilantro to the bowl and mix together well.

Spoon the mixture onto a plate. Sometimes a loose presentation is nice, but if you want to serve it like a traditional tartare, use a chef's ring as a mold, and press the tuna mixture down firmly so it holds its shape.

To serve, remove the ring, if using, and scatter over a few sesame seeds and some extra cilantro.

TIP SESAME OIL IS WONDERFULLY RICH IN FLAVOR. HOWEVER, A LITTLE GOES A LONG WAY, SO ADD JUST A LITTLE AT A TIME, AND TASTE AS YOU GO.

If you have ever been to Italy, you will realize that the simplest dishes can be the best. It's all about the produce, so look for the best-quality beef, and the freshest, most peppery arugula, and enjoy this delicious, classic dish.

BEEF CARPACCIO
WITH WALNUT OIL

246 calories | 17.3g fat | 3.9g saturates | 0.8g sugar | 0.1g salt | 21.6g protein | 0.6g fiber

Serves 4 as an appetizer

14 oz beef tenderloin
4 tablespoons walnut oil
freshly ground black
    pepper
7 oz arugula leaves
2 lemons, cut into wedges

Place the beef in the freezer for 30 minutes before you are ready to serve, as this will firm it up and make it easier to slice thinly.

Using a very sharp knife, slice the beef as thinly as you can.

Lay each slice of beef on a chopping board, cover with plastic wrap, and using a rolling pin, stretch and roll the beef until it is as thin as it will go.

Remove the plastic wrap, and divide the beef between four serving plates. Drizzle each one with a tablespoon of walnut oil, and season with a few grinds of black pepper. Serve with arugula and lemon wedges on the side.

TIP BEEF IS PROTEIN-RICH AND CRITICAL FOR MUSCLE GROWTH AND RECOVERY. IT ALSO CONTAINS HIGH AMOUNTS OF IRON AND VITAMIN B12, WHICH BOOST THE IMMUNE SYSTEM, AND KEEP THE RED BLOOD CELLS HEALTHY.

Ceviche is the classic South American way to prepare raw fish. It is marinated in citrus juices, and the acidity cures the fish, which has the same effect as cooking it, but in a way that preserves all its fresh flavor.

SCALLOP CEVICHE
WITH FRESH HERBS

180 calories | 11.9g fat | 1.8g saturates | 1.6g sugar | 0.3g salt | 14.7g protein | 0.4g fiber

Serves 4

9 oz fresh raw scallops
juice of 1 lemon
4 tablespoons olive oil
2 scallions, finely
   chopped
½ small red onion, finely
   chopped
1 red bird's eye chili,
   finely chopped (seeds
   removed if you don't
   want it hot)
a handful of cilantro
   leaves, to garnish
6–8 fresh basil leaves,
   thinly sliced
freshly ground black
   pepper

Using a sharp knife, slice each scallop into about three thin discs. Arrange these in a single layer on a large serving plate.

In a bowl, mix together the lemon juice and olive oil. Add the scallions, onion, and chili, and stir to combine.

Pour the dressing over the scallops, and set aside to marinate for at least 20 minutes. Scatter over the fresh cilantro and basil, and season with a few grinds of black pepper.

TIP AS THE FISH HERE IS NOT COOKED WITH HEAT, IT IS ESSENTIAL THAT YOU USE FISH THAT IS AS FRESH AS POSSIBLE, AND WORK WITH VERY CLEAN HANDS, UTENSILS, AND SURFACES.

I first made this pâté to go on toasted bread, but discovered it's just as good with fresh, crunchy vegetables. Serve this with carrot and celery crudités for a light lunch, or as a great way to start a dinner party.

TUNA AND
OLIVE PÂTÉ

314 calories | 16.8g fat | 2.3g saturates | 0.4g sugar | 2.7g salt | 40.2g protein | 2g fiber

Serves 4

20 oz canned tuna in
   water, drained
1 tablespoon capers
1 tablespoon chopped
   tarragon
12 fresh basil leaves,
   plus extra to garnish
2 oz canned anchovies,
   drained
5 oz pitted black olives,
   drained
1 tablespoon Dijon
   mustard
juice of ½ lemon
3 tablespoons olive oil

Place all the ingredients in a food processor, and blend until smooth.

Divide the pâté mix between four ramekins, and refrigerate for at least 30 minutes.

Garnish with fresh basil, and serve with freshly prepared carrot and celery crudités.

TIP TARRAGON IS RICH IN VITAMIN C, AND HELPS BOOST THE IMMUNE SYSTEM. IT IS A GREAT HERB TO HAVE ON HAND, AND GOES PARTICULARLY WELL WITH MANY TYPES OF FISH (SEE THE RECIPE FOR TUNA WITH OLIVE TAPENADE ON PAGE 119).

This is the kind of meal you get in the Florida Keys — sitting at an old bar on the water, enjoying a beer and a cheap, simple meal of fresh seafood. I know beer is not allowed on the Paleo diet, but this recipe is to enjoy with friends, al fresco.

STEAMED CLAMS
WITH LEMON AND HERBS

328 calories | 12.3g fat | 2.3g saturates | 0.2g sugar | 2.8g salt | 45.5g protein | 0g fiber

Serves 4

6 dozen clams
4 garlic cloves, chopped
¼ cup vegetable bouillon
2 tablespoons olive oil
4 tablespoons shredded
   fresh basil
2 tablespoons chopped
   flat-leaf parsley
juice of 1 lemon
freshly ground black
   pepper

Clean your clams in a colander and rinse well. Add to a large stockpot with the garlic and bouillon, bring to a boil, and cover. Cook for 4–5 minutes over medium heat, or until the clams open. Discard any that remain closed.

Add the oil, herbs, and lemon juice. Mix in well, season with black pepper and serve.

TIP CLAMS ARE A GREAT LEAN PROTEIN AS A 3 OZ SERVING CONTAINS 20G PROTEIN AND ONLY 2G FAT. THIS IS ABOUT THE SAME AS CHICKEN, THOUGH CLAMS ARE FAR MORE NUTRIENT-RICH.

The key to making this dish great is to use the best crab you can. If you are using canned, you will find you have about three options in the supermarket in terms of cost and quality, and I'd recommend you buy the most expensive, as it really makes a difference to the end result here.

ASIAN FUSION
CRAB CAKES

372 calories | 29.2g fat | 4.2g saturates | 1.4g sugar | 1.3g salt | 25.7g protein | 0.9g fiber

Serves 4

1 red bird's eye chili
1 garlic clove, peeled
½ small onion
a handful of cilantro, plus extra to garnish
1 tablespoon almond flour
1 egg, plus 1 egg white
1 lb fresh crabmeat (or premium canned)
1 tablespoon sesame oil
juice of 1 lime or lemon
freshly ground black pepper
3–4 tablespoons olive oil
3½ oz arugula leaves

for the dressing
juice of ½ lemon
3 tablespoons olive oil
a few grinds of black pepper

Place the chili, garlic, onion, cilantro, almond flour, egg, and egg white in a food processor and blend until smooth.

Transfer this spice and herb mix to a large bowl, and add three-quarters of the crabmeat, along with the sesame oil, and lime or lemon juice. Season with black pepper, and stir thoroughly to combine. (Don't be tempted to place all the ingredients in the food processor, as otherwise the fish cakes will have no texture and you'll miss the wonderful flakes of crab.) Add the remaining crabmeat, and stir into the mixture.

Divide the mixture into four portions. On a clean surface, carefully shape into four cakes about 1 inch thick. Transfer to a plate, cover, and chill for 30 minutes (or up to a day).

Meanwhile, mix the dressing ingredients together, and set aside.

Heat the olive oil in a large, nonstick sauté pan over high heat, and cook the fish cakes for 2–3 minutes on each side.

Serve with arugula leaves, a scattering of chopped cilantro, and a drizzle of the lemon and olive oil dressing.

I first realized this recipe was a winner for kids when I made it for my eldest daughter, Eleanor. She loved it instantly, and I've made it for her and her friends over and over again. You might want to reduce the chili quantity a little for a younger crowd, but I guarantee you, it will be a hit.

SALMON

FISH CAKES

444 calories | 29.4g fat | 5.1g saturates | 1.8g sugar | 0.4g salt | 43.1g protein | 1.1g fiber

Serves 4

1¾ lb salmon fillets, roughly chopped

1 red chili, roughly chopped

2 scallions, finely chopped

½ red onion, finely chopped

juice of 1 lime or ½ lemon

1 egg

1-inch piece of fresh ginger, grated

a handful of cilantro leaves, plus extra to garnish

2 tablespoons olive oil

3½ oz spinach leaves

1 lemon, cut into wedges

Place the salmon, chili, scallions, red onion, lime or lemon juice, egg, ginger, and cilantro in a food processor, and blitz together, making sure you retain a little texture.

Divide the fish cake mixture into four portions. On a clean surface, carefully shape into four cakes about 1 inch thick. Transfer to a plate, cover, and chill for 30 minutes (or up to a day).

Heat the olive oil in a large, nonstick sauté pan over high heat, and cook the fish cakes for 2–3 minutes on each side.

Serve with spinach leaves, a scattering of chopped cilantro, and a squeeze of lemon.

TIP WILD SALMON IS ALWAYS PREFERABLE TO FARMED SALMON, AS THE LATTER MAY HAVE BEEN INJECTED WITH ANTIBIOTICS AND COLOR-ENHANCING CHEMICALS.

Mushrooms have such a meaty texture, and are so substantial, that you won't even notice this is a vegetarian dish. The almond flour adds a lovely crunch and texture, but keeps it tasting light and fresh — a perfect quick and easy lunch.

PORTOBELLO MUSHROOMS WITH ALMOND CRUST

629 calories | 58.2g fat | 5.7g saturates | 4.7g sugar | 0.1g salt | 19.2g protein | 6.8g fiber

Serves 2

4 portobello mushrooms, stems cut out
½ cup almonds
¾ cup almond flour
a few sprigs of flat-leaf parsley, plus extra to garnish
1 garlic clove, peeled
3 tablespoons olive oil
freshly ground black pepper
5 oz mixed salad leaves
1 lemon, cut into wedges

Preheat the oven to 450°F.

Wipe the mushrooms clean with a paper towel (do not use water, as this will make them slimy).

In a food processor, blend the almonds, almond flour, parsley, and garlic. Transfer this mixture to a wide, shallow bowl, add 2 tablespoons of the olive oil, season and mix together well.

Dip the top of each mushroom into the almond mix, pressing down to coat well, then place on a baking sheet. Divide the rest of the mixture between each mushroom, and drizzle the remaining olive oil on top.

Bake in the oven for 15–18 minutes, until the almond crust is crispy and golden.

Serve on a pile of salad leaves with a wedge of lemon, and an extra sprinkling of chopped parsley.

There are so many restaurants that serve calamari, and so often it's deep-fried, greasy, and high in saturated fat. However, it doesn't have to be that way, and this recipe gives you a lighter, better-tasting version with far less fat. You can also try it with fish fillets — equally tasty!

LIGHT FRIED
CALAMARI

349 calories | 22.3g fat | 3g saturates | 0.7g sugar | 0.6g salt | 34g protein | 1.5g fiber

Serves 4

1¾ lb cleaned squid, cut into rings
4 tablespoons almond flour
freshly ground black pepper
4 tablespoons olive oil
1 lemon, cut into wedges

Place the squid in a large ziplock bag, add the flour and a few grinds of black pepper, and shake well so there is a light coating on all the squid. Do this in batches, if you like.

Heat 1 tablespoon of the oil in a large pan over high heat, and add a quarter of the squid. Cook for a minute, then reduce the heat to medium and toss the squid for another 2–3 minutes — turning it over and over until golden brown. Remove the squid and set aside. Repeat in three further batches until you have cooked all the squid.

Serve the calamari with a lemon wedge on the side.

TIP CALAMARI IS ONE OF THE LEANEST AND MOST DELICIOUS TYPES OF SEA-DERIVED PROTEIN, PLUS IT'S OFTEN ONE OF THE CHEAPEST, TOO.

Tahini is a Middle-Eastern ingredient: a thick paste made from ground sesame seeds that is traditionally added to hummus. However, as chickpeas are not part of the Paleo plan, I've created the next best thing and matched sesame seeds with eggplants. You can try this with acorn squash, too, but don't forget the garlic — it's a must.

EGGPLANT
TAHINI DIP

337 calories | 30.5g fat | 4.9g saturates | 9.2g sugar | 0.2g salt | 6.3g protein | 9.9g fiber

Serves 4

2 large eggplants, halved
6 tablespoons olive oil
freshly ground black pepper
6 tablespoons sesame seeds
2 garlic cloves, peeled
freshly chopped flat-leaf parsley, to garnish
10¾ oz carrots, peeled, and cut into sticks
10¾ oz celery, cut into sticks

Preheat the oven to 375°F.

Prick the eggplants with a fork and place, cut-side up, on a roasting pan. Drizzle with 1 tablespoon of the olive oil, and bake in the oven for 20 minutes, until the skin is charred and the flesh is soft.

When the eggplant is cooked, scoop out the flesh and place in a food processor. Add the remaining ingredients (except the crudités), along with the rest of the olive oil and blend until smooth.

Scoop the dip into a bowl, sprinkle over some chopped parsley, and serve with crunchy celery and carrot crudités.

TIP TAHINI — GROUND SESAME SEEDS — IS A STAR INGREDIENT, CONTAINING MORE PROTEIN THAN MILK AND MOST NUTS. IT'S ALSO A RICH SOURCE OF B VITAMINS THAT BOOST ENERGY AND BRAIN FUNCTION, AND IMPORTANT MINERALS SUCH AS MAGNESIUM, IRON, AND CALCIUM.

VARIATION TAHINI ALSO MAKES A LOVELY DRESSING FOR SALADS AND GRILLED MEATS. MIX 3 TABLESPOONS TAHINI WITH 2 TABLESPOONS WATER, 1 TABLESPOON LEMON JUICE, AND ½ CLOVE CRUSHED GARLIC.

Being on a diet doesn't mean you can't snack. You can never eat enough vegetables, and these dips just make them a little more interesting. Enjoy as much and as often as you like!

CRUDITÉS WITH SUN-DRIED TOMATO AND OLIVE OIL DIPS

570 calories | 54.7g fat | 8g saturates | 10.6g sugar | 1.4g salt | 7.7g protein | 7.1g fiber

Serves 4

10¾ oz carrots, peeled
  and cut into sticks
10¾ oz celery, cut into
  sticks
10¾ oz raw broccoli
  florets
10¾ oz cherry tomatoes

for the tomato dip

6½ oz sun-dried
  tomatoes in olive oil
1 garlic clove, crushed
2 tablespoons chopped
  basil
5 tablespoons olive oil

for the olive oil dip

2 egg yolks
6 tablespoons olive oil
1 tablespoon chopped
  tarragon
1 garlic clove, peeled

Arrange all the vegetables on a large platter.

FOR THE TOMATO DIP:
Drain the tomatoes from the oil they are in, as this is too strong in flavor. Place them in a blender with the remaining ingredients, and blend until smooth. Scoop into a serving dish, and serve with the vegetables.

FOR THE OLIVE OIL DIP:
Place the egg yolks in a blender, and start the motor. Slowly add the oil as a trickle — as you would when making a mayonnaise — and gradually incorporate it all. Add the tarragon and garlic, and blitz until smooth. Serve in a dish alongside the vegetables.

TIP MYTH HAS IT THAT CELERY IS JUST WATER — IT'S NOT! IT ALSO CONTAINS A UNIQUE COMBINATION OF DISEASE-PREVENTING VITAMINS, MINERALS, AND PHYTOCHEMICALS. HOWEVER, IT IS TRUE THAT IT IS VIRTUALLY CALORIE-FREE: 1 STICK CONTAINS 1G FIBER AND ABOUT 10 CALORIES!

This is a great crowd-pleasing canapé to make for a drinks party. Serve this while dinner is being made, and your guests will love it.

SPICY GUACAMOLE BLINIS

435 calories | 38g fat | 5.4g saturates | 1.7g sugar | 0.1g salt | 14.7g protein | 16.1g fiber

Serves 12

for the blinis
2 cups almond flour
5 scant cups flaxseed meal
2 eggs, beaten
generous ¾ cup water
2 tablespoons olive oil

for the guacamole
3 large ripe avocados, halved, pitted and cubed
a handful of fresh cilantro, chopped, plus extra to garnish
2 large tomatoes, seeded and chopped
4 tablespoons olive oil
1 small bird's eye chili, finely chopped
juice of 1 lemon or lime

a few chives, chopped, to garnish

First make the blinis. In a large mixing bowl, stir together the flour, meal, eggs, and water to make a batter.

Heat the oil in a nonstick frying pan over medium heat, and in batches, drop spoonfuls of the batter into the hot pan to make blini-style pancakes. Cook until the surface starts to bubble (1–2 minutes), and then flip over to cook the other side. Set aside to cool on a plate.

Now make the guacamole. Spoon the avocado into a mixing bowl. Add the cilantro and all the remaining guacamole ingredients and thoroughly combine.

Spoon a little guacamole onto each blini, and top with a scattering of fresh chives, and extra cilantro.

TIP FLAXSEEDS ARE INCREDIBLY NUTRITIOUS — RICH IN FIBER, OMEGA-3 FATTY ACIDS, AND ESSENTIAL NUTRIENTS. HOWEVER, WHEN GROUND INTO MEAL, THEY'RE EASIER TO DIGEST, AND SO ARE EVEN BETTER FOR YOU!

We all get cravings for pizza, so here is the best Paleo-friendly way to satisfy them. Sometimes the simplest toppings are the best, and here, you'll see, a delicious cheese-free pesto is all you need.

PESTO
PIZZA

416 calories | 40.8g fat | 5g saturates | 1.4g sugar | 0.1g salt | 10g protein | 2.7g fiber

Serves 4

1 cup almond flour
2 eggs
3 fl oz water
3 tablespoons olive oil

for the topping
4 tablespoons olive oil
1 garlic clove, peeled
a large handful of basil
  leaves
⅔ cup pine nuts

Preheat the oven to 375°F.

In a large mixing bowl, whisk the almond flour, eggs, water, and olive oil together. When the mixture starts to resemble a dough, use your hands to knead it a little, but be gentle, as this will crumble more than normal flour dough.

To make the pesto topping, combine the oil, garlic, basil, and pine nuts in a blender, and blitz until smooth.

Divide the dough mixture in half, and using your hands rather than a rolling pin, flatten out into two pizza shapes on parchment paper, or on two nonstick pizza pans. Top with the pesto, spreading the sauce out almost to the edges.

Cook the pizzas in the oven for 12 minutes, then turn off the heat and finish off for an additional 3–4 minutes.

Be creative with your choice of toppings — olives are great on pizza, and so is fish and seafood. The Italians are pretty strict on their "no cheese with fish" rule, and so Neptune pizzas are traditionally cheese-free anyway.

BLACK OLIVE
PIZZA

465 calories | 46.3g fat | 5.8g saturates | 1.2g sugar | 1.3g salt | 10g protein | 6.2g fiber

Serves 4

1 cup almond flour
2 eggs
3 fl oz water
3 tablespoons olive oil

for the topping
12 oz black pitted
  olives, drained
1 garlic clove, peeled
a handful of basil
  leaves
1 tablespoon pine nuts
2 tablespoons olive oil

Preheat the oven to 375°F.

In a large mixing bowl, whisk the almond flour, eggs, water, and olive oil together. When the mixture starts to resemble a dough, use your hands to knead it a little, but be gentle, as this will crumble more than normal flour dough.

Place all the topping ingredients in a blender, and blend to a chunky consistency.

Divide the dough mixture in half, and using your hands rather than a rolling pin, flatten out into two pizza shapes on parchment paper, or on two nonstick pizza pans. Top with the olive mixture, spreading it out almost to the edges.

Cook the pizzas in the oven for 12 minutes, then turn off the heat and finish off for an additional 3–4 minutes.

I love when I create a healthy dish that doesn't feel "diet" at all, and this is one of those — pure decadence. I always remember being taken to a very expensive restaurant in New York, and inhaling the aroma, which filled the entire place when white truffles were being shaved over pasta.

GRILLED ARTICHOKES
WITH WHITE TRUFFLE MAYO

260 calories | 26.3g fat | 4.3g saturates | 1.1g sugar | 0g salt | 4.6g protein | 1g fiber

Serves 4

4 large globe artichoke hearts, trimmed and halved
4 tablespoons olive oil
1 garlic clove, crushed
1 tablespoon chopped fresh mixed herbs, like rosemary and thyme
1 lemon, cut into wedges

for the truffle mayo
3 egg yolks
4 tablespoons white truffle oil

Place the artichokes in a large saucepan of boiling water, and simmer over medium heat for 20 minutes.

Combine the olive oil, garlic, and herbs in a small bowl, and set aside to infuse.

Meanwhile, make the truffle mayo dip. This is just like a mayonnaise, so place the egg yolks in a bowl and whisk with an electric whisk as you drizzle in the truffle oil. Very slowly incorporate it all so it thickens.

Drain the artichokes, and place on paper towels to absorb any water. Now heat a griddle pan (or the barbecue), and lightly brush the artichokes with the infused garlic and herb oil. Cook for 3–5 minutes on each side.

Serve with the white truffle mayonnaise and lemon wedges to squeeze over.

TIP ARTICHOKES ARE PACKED WITH ANTIOXIDANTS, MAKING THEM INCREDIBLE DEFENDERS AGAINST CANCER, AGING, HEART DISEASE, AND ILLNESS.

One Christmas, I was experimenting with trying to cook parsnips in a different way, and I came up with this recipe. Now I eat parsnip purée all year long. It's especially good served under seared scallops with a red wine reduction. Not strictly Paleo, but perfect for a treat day.

PARSNIP PURÉE

489 calories | 36.3g fat | 5.3g saturates | 16.5g sugar | 0.1g salt | 5.4g protein | 18.4g fiber

Serves 2

1 whole head of garlic
6 tablespoons olive oil,
    plus extra for drizzling
6 large parsnips, peeled

Preheat the oven to 450°F.

Peel away the outer layers of the garlic head, leaving the skin of the individual bulbs intact. With a sharp knife, slice the very top off the garlic head, then wrap it in a piece of foil, leaving an opening at the top. Drizzle 1 tablespoon of the olive oil over the head, and seal tightly. Roast in the oven for 40 minutes (or until the cloves feel soft and squishy).

Fill a saucepan with water, and bring it to a boil. Slice each parsnip into 4–5 pieces, and then cook over medium heat for 20 minutes.

Drain the parsnips, transfer to a food processor and add the remaining olive oil.

Take the roasted garlic out of the oven and allow to cool slightly. Squeeze about half of the garlic cloves out of their skin, and place in the food processor. Blitz until smooth.

To serve, spoon the purée onto plates, drizzle with a little oil, and accompany with a few of the roasted garlic cloves on the side.

TIP ROASTED GARLIC IS DELICIOUS AS THE LONG COOKING PROCESS REDUCES ITS PUNGENCY, MAKING IT SWEET, STICKY, AND GOLDEN, WITH THE TEXTURE OF BUTTER.

This dish is great as a side to go with any Red recipe.
Red onions take on a wonderful sweet flavor when cooked, and
I love to contrast this with the addition of fresh green herbs.

CARAMELIZED ONIONS

249 calories | 11.4g fat | 1.6g saturates | 32.5g sugar | trace salt | 2.3g protein | 3.3g fiber

Serves 4

4 tablespoons olive oil
6 red onions, finely sliced
¼ cup vegetable bouillon
6 tablespoons raw honey
freshly ground black
   pepper
chopped fresh herbs
   (flat-leaf parsley
   and thyme work
   particularly well)

Heat 2 tablespoons of the oil in a large, nonstick frying pan over high heat. Add the onions, and cook, tossing continuously, for 2–3 minutes. Add the remaining olive oil, and cook for an additional 3–4 minutes, until the onions have turned a dark, rich brown color (this is the sugar in the onion caramelizing).

Add the bouillon and honey to the pan, and reduce the temperature to low. Cook for 5–6 minutes, until the liquid has been absorbed and the onions have caramelized.

Season with a few grinds of black pepper, and increase the heat for a final few minutes.

Stir through the fresh herbs and serve immediately.

When I tried out this tempura for the book, I was so happy with the results, that I immediately shared the recipe with friends. I also recommend that you try it with other vegetables, like eggplant or carrots, and large shrimp, too.

CRISPY VEGETABLE
TEMPURA

199 calories | 17.7g fat | 8.4g saturates | 2.2g sugar | 0.1g salt | 7.3g protein | 2.4g fiber

Serves 6

6–8 large zucchini,
   topped and tailed
1 cup almond flour
6 tablespoons almond or
   coconut oil, for frying
3 eggs

Slice your zucchini into thin slices, and pat with kitchen towels to remove any moisture — they must be completely dry. Set aside.

Place the almond flour on a large serving plate and set aside. Heat the oil in a large wok to 375°F.

Whisk the eggs in a large bowl, and then dip in the zucchini, about 3–4 slices at a time.

Now dip the zucchini in the almond flour, ensuring they are thoroughly coated.

In batches, fry the zucchini slices in the hot oil for 2–3 minutes until golden and puffy. Drain on kitchen towels, and continue to work through the remaining tempura.

Season with pepper and serve.

TIP DON'T BE TEMPTED TO USE OLIVE OIL, AS IT'S NOT GOOD FOR FRYING AT HIGH TEMPERATURES. ALMOND OR COCONUT OILS ARE BETTER FOR THIS PURPOSE.

We always remember how much we love Brussels sprouts at Christmas time, but in my view, it's criminal to neglect them throughout the rest of the year. This is my favorite way to cook them, as the dish is full of great texture, and the sprouts never become mushy.

ROASTED BRUSSELS SPROUTS WITH CHESTNUTS

455 calories | 29.3g fat | 4.5g saturates | 10.9g sugar | 0.1g salt | 12g protein | 13.3g fiber

Serves 6

1¾ lb Brussels sprouts, trimmed
1 lb canned chestnuts, quartered
½ cup unsalted cashews, roughly chopped
1 red onion, peeled and quartered
4 tablespoons almond oil
1 tablespoon olive oil
½ cup unsalted walnuts
scant ½ cup toasted pumpkin seeds
freshly ground black pepper

Preheat the oven to 450°F.

Place all the ingredients in a large mixing bowl, toss together, and season with black pepper.

Tip everything into a roasting pan, and roast in the oven for 20–25 minutes, tossing thoroughly halfway through the cooking time.

TIP THIS IS A GREAT DISH SERVED ON ITS OWN AS A VEGETARIAN LUNCH. FEEL FREE TO ADD A FEW EXTRA PECANS OR CASHEWS TO THE CHESTNUTS.

VARIATION I ALSO LOVE ROASTING CARROTS AND PARSNIPS TOGETHER WITH A LITTLE OLIVE OIL, A FEW SPRIGS OF ROSEMARY, AND A LIGHT DRIZZLE OF HONEY. COOK AS ABOVE BUT FOR SLIGHTLY LONGER — ABOUT 40 MINUTES, TOSSING EVERY 10 MINUTES OR SO.

This is a great side dish with any mains that are marked Red.
Spinach is a great source of iron and the coconut milk gives this a similar
texture to creamed spinach.

COCONUT SPINACH
WITH CHOPPED ALMONDS

111 calories | 9.2g fat | 2.2g saturates | 2g sugar | 0.4g salt | 4.5g protein | 2.8g fiber

Serves 4

1 tablespoon olive oil
14 oz spinach
4–6 tablespoons light
   coconut milk
2 tablespoons roughly
   chopped almonds
freshly ground black
   pepper

Heat the olive oil in a large pan over high heat, and add the spinach.
Fry for 2–3 minutes, stirring constantly.

Add the coconut milk, and simmer for 2 minutes, then add the almonds,
stir through, and serve with a twist of black pepper.

SOUPS &
SALADS

Chilled soups are wonderfully refreshing, and so perfect for a hot summer's day, or even after a hard day at the office, when you want something light and simple in the evening. The creaminess of the avocado gives this soup a wonderful texture — try it!

CHILLED AVOCADO
SOUP

313 calories | 30g fat | 6.3g saturates | 0.8g sugar | 0.1g salt | 7.8g protein | 6.8g fiber

Serves 4

4 ripe avocados, halved and pitted

1⅔ cups cold vegetable bouillon

3½ oz salmon roe (optional)

2 tablespoons chopped chives

freshly ground black pepper

Scoop the avocado flesh into a food processor, add the cold vegetable bouillon, and blend until smooth. Chill the soup in the refrigerator for at least 30 minutes.

Divide the chilled soup between four bowls, and serve with a scoop of salmon roe (if using), a scattering of chopped chives, and a twist of black pepper.

TIP IF YOU ARE WATCHING YOUR WEIGHT AND YOUR FAT INTAKE, REDUCE THE AMOUNT OF AVOCADO BY HALF. THE TEXTURE WILL BE LESS CREAMY, BUT THE FLAVOR WILL STILL BE THERE.

This soup can be served hot or cold. Serving it cold has a similar
taste to a French Vichyssoise — a thick soup made of puréed leeks, potatoes,
and cream. In fact, you can pan-fry a little shredded leek for a few
minutes, and add to the soup as a garnish.

ASPARAGUS
SOUP

90 calories | 6.4g fat | 0.9g saturates | 3.3g sugar | 0g salt | 4.1g protein | 2.7g fiber

Serves 4

2 tablespoons olive oil
1 onion, finely chopped
14 oz asparagus,
trimmed
2¼ cups vegetable
bouillon
a handful of chives,
chopped
freshly ground black
pepper

Heat the oil in a large saucepan, and sauté the onion over medium heat for 3–5 minutes.

Chop each asparagus spear into thirds, and add to the pan with the onion, sautéing for 2–3 minutes. Add the bouillon, and simmer for 12–15 minutes.

Turn off the heat, and allow to cool slightly before blending the soup with a hand blender until smooth.

Return the soup to a saucepan, and place back on medium heat to warm through. Serve with a sprinkling of fresh chives, and a twist or two of freshly ground black pepper.

TIP THE SEASON FOR FRESH ASPARAGUS IS VERY SHORT, SO MAKE SURE YOU MAKE THE MOST OF IT BY COOKING THIS INCREDIBLY FLAVORSOME SOUP.

This soup is not quite as simple as the other ones in this chapter, but it is worth every effort. I often make double quantities and freeze a batch. That way, you can also use it as a stock for cooking a quick seafood or fish supper.

FISH SOUP OR FRENCH BOUILLABAISSE

182 calories | 10g fat | 1.6g saturates | 1.4g sugar | 1.8g salt | 20.3g protein | 0.4g fiber

Serves 6

3 tablespoons olive oil
2 garlic cloves, finely
    chopped
1 quart fish bouillon
4 tablespoons tomato
    paste
4 tablespoons sun-dried
    tomato paste
7 oz skinless salmon
    fillet, cut into chunks
7 oz skinless monkfish
    fillet, cut into chunks
15 small scallops
16 tiger shrimp, peeled
20 clams
20 mussels
a handful of chives,
    chopped
freshly ground black
    pepper

Heat the oil in a large saucepan over medium heat, and fry the garlic for 30 seconds. Add the bouillon and tomato pastes, and bring to a simmer. Cover with a lid, and simmer gently for 15 minutes.

Add all the fish and seafood and cook, uncovered, for 4–5 minutes, or until the fish is cooked and the clams and mussels have opened. Discard any shells that remain closed.

Serve with a scattering of chives, and a twist of black pepper.

> **TIP** SCALLOPS ARE ALMOST 80% PROTEIN, PLUS THEY'RE A RICH SOURCE OF VITAMIN B12, MAGNESIUM, POTASSIUM, AND MANY OTHER NUTRIENTS.

A traditional French onion soup is served with a toasted slice
of baguette smothered in Gruyère, and while very tasty, is neither healthy,
nor part of the Paleo plan! However, this recipe is both those things, plus
it retains all the flavor and restorative umami of the French classic.

ONION AND THYME
SOUP

150 calories | 9.1g fat | 1.2g saturates | 9.6g sugar | 0.2g salt | 4g protein | 3.3g fiber

Serves 4

3 tablespoons olive oil
4 large onions, peeled
    and finely sliced
approx. 1 tablespoon
    fresh thyme leaves
3 garlic cloves, crushed
1 bay leaf
1 quart good-quality
    vegetable bouillon
chopped flat-leaf parsley,
    to garnish
freshly ground black
    pepper

In a large cast-iron casserole dish or saucepan, heat the oil over low
heat, and gently cook the onion and thyme until the onion is softened
but not browned — about 20 minutes. Increase the heat slightly and
cook for 15 minutes, until the onion becomes dark golden, sticky, and
caramelized, stirring now and then to stop it sticking. Add the garlic
and cook, stirring, for a few minutes.

Add the bay leaf and bouillon, and bring to a boil. Season, and simmer
for 15 minutes. Serve with a scattering of fresh parsley, and a twist
of black pepper.

TIP FOUR MAY SEEM LIKE A LOT, BUT COOKING THE ONIONS FOR THIS
LENGTH OF TIME MEANS THAT THEY LOSE THEIR PUNGENCY — I PROMISE!

TIP FOR THIS SOUP, MAKE SURE YOU HAVE A REALLY GOOD-QUALITY
VEGETABLE BOUILLON, AS IT WILL MAKE ALL THE DIFFERENCE TO THE
SOUP'S DEPTH OF FLAVOR.

The key to this soup is to include a really good mix of mushrooms. Shiitake mushrooms are always great, but you can use almost anything, from small button mushrooms through to soaked, dried porcini — the latter always provide an excellent depth of flavor.

MIXED MUSHROOM

SOUP

159 calories | 14g fat | 5.8g saturates | 2.9g sugar | 0.2g salt | 3.8g protein | 2.2g fiber

Serves 4

2 tablespoons olive oil

1 white onion, finely chopped

14 oz mixed mushrooms, sliced

3 garlic cloves, crushed

2½ cups vegetable bouillon

scant 1 cup light coconut milk

finely chopped flat-leaf parsley, to garnish

freshly ground black pepper

Heat the oil in a saucepan over high heat, and sweat the onion for 3–4 minutes. Add all the mushrooms, reduce the heat and cook, stirring, for an additional few minutes.

Add the garlic and bouillon, and simmer for 15 minutes, then add the coconut milk, and cook for another minute to fuse the flavors.

Turn off the heat, and allow to cool slightly, before blending the soup with a hand blender until smooth.

Return the soup to a saucepan, and place back on medium heat to warm through.

Serve with a sprinkling of fresh parsley, and a twist of black pepper.

TIP MUSHROOMS ARE INCREASINGLY BEING HAILED AS A SUPERFOOD — THEY CONTAIN VIRTUALLY NO FAT, SUGAR, OR SALT, PLUS THEY'RE A GOOD SOURCE OF DIETARY FIBER, AS WELL AS ALL FIVE B VITAMINS.

Coconut and beets might seem like a surprising combination, but trust me, it works. The finished soup is also a wonderful color — a beautiful, vibrant pink — so I find it's a great way to start a dinner party.

COCONUT BEET

SOUP

219 calories | 15.8g fat | 9.8g saturates | 11.7g sugar | 0.2g salt | 4.7g protein | 3.9g fiber

Serves 4

18 oz beets
3 bay leaves
few sprigs of oregano
2 tablespoons olive oil
1 red onion, finely
   chopped
3 cups vegetable bouillon
14 fl oz light coconut
   milk
freshly ground black
   pepper
finely chopped flat-leaf
   parsley, to garnish

Cook the beets in boiling salted water with the bay leaves and oregano for 50–60 minutes. Take off the heat, and let cool in the water. When cool enough to handle, peel and roughly chop.

Heat the olive oil in a large saucepan over medium heat, and sweat the onion for 3–4 minutes. Add the beets, and toss in the oil. Add the bouillon, and simmer, covered, for 15 minutes. Add the coconut milk, and simmer, uncovered, for 2–3 minutes. Season with black pepper, and take off the heat.

Transfer to a blender, and purée until smooth. Return to a saucepan, and warm through.

Spoon into serving bowls, and finish with a scattering of fresh parsley.

TIP BEETS HAVE A MEDIUM GI (GLYCEMIC INDEX) OF 64, BUT A VERY LOW GL (GLYCEMIC LOAD) OF 2.9, WHICH MEANS IT'S CONVERTED INTO SUGARS VERY SLOWLY, AND THEREFORE KEEPS BLOOD SUGAR LEVELS NICE AND STABLE.

Pumpkin is a starchy form of carbohydrate, but much less so than potato, sweet potato, or yams, so it is fine in moderation. I find it a wonderful ingredient for soup, as it creates a rich, thick texture, but with a lovely, delicate sweetness.

ROASTED PUMPKIN SOUP

173 calories | 14.6g fat | 7.2g saturates | 5.2g sugar | 0.2g salt | 3.2g protein | 2.8g fiber

Serves 6

1 medium pumpkin
7 tablespoons olive oil
1 whole head of garlic
1 onion, finely chopped
4½ cups vegetable bouillon
14 fl oz light coconut milk
4 tablespoons pumpkin seeds
fresh thyme leaves, to garnish (optional)

Preheat the oven to 425°F.

Cut the top off the pumpkin, scoop out the seeds and fibers and discard. Cut the pumpkin into 4 quarters, and place on a baking sheet. Drizzle over 4 tablespoons of the olive oil.

Slice the top off the head of garlic, and drizzle over 1 tablespoon of the olive oil. Wrap in foil (so it is completely sealed), place on the baking sheet with the pumpkin, then roast in the hot oven for 45 minutes.

Heat 1 tablespoon of the olive oil in a large saucepan, and gently fry the onion for a few minutes. Add the vegetable bouillon, and bring to a simmer, then cover, and take off the heat.

When the pumpkin is cooked, discard the skin, and add the flesh to the saucepan. Squeeze the garlic flesh out of the skins, and add to the pot, along with the coconut milk. Bring the contents to a boil, and cook for 10 minutes on medium heat.

Remove the pan from the heat, and set aside to cool slightly, before puréeing the soup in a food processor until velvety and smooth.

Heat the remaining tablespoon of oil in a frying pan over medium heat, and fry the pumpkin seeds for 1–2 minutes until just toasted. To serve, reheat the soup, and garnish with the toasted pumpkin seeds, and fresh thyme leaves, if using.

This is the perfect lunch for a cold winter's day. If you like a thick, filling bowl of soup, use a little less bouillon, and roughly blend the vegetables so you don't smooth out all the texture.

BROCCOLI AND PARSNIP SOUP

196 calories | 10.8g fat | 1.6g saturates | 9.1g sugar | 0.4g salt | 8.2g protein | 10.3g fiber

Serves 4

3 tablespoons olive oil
1 white onion, chopped
4 parsnips, 3½ peeled
   and chopped (½ thinly
   sliced or shaved and
   reserved for later)
14 oz broccoli florets
3 garlic cloves, crushed
1 quart vegetable
   bouillon
freshly ground black
   pepper

Heat 2 tablespoons of the oil in a large saucepan over medium heat, and sweat the onion for 2–3 minutes.

Add the parsnips (except the half set aside), broccoli, and garlic to the pot and stir. Cover with the bouillon, and simmer for 25 minutes (or until the parsnips are tender). Remove from the heat.

Using a blender or hand-held blender, blend the vegetables until smooth.

Heat the remaining tablespoon of olive oil in a nonstick frying pan, and fry the reserved parsnip shavings until they become crisp and golden.

Pour the soup into a saucepan, season with black pepper, then heat until barely simmering.

Remove from the heat, divide between your serving bowls, and garnish with a few parsnip chips.

TIP BROCCOLI IS A TRUE SUPERFOOD, AND CONTAINS MORE NUTRIENTS THAN ANY OTHER VEGETABLE. EAT IT AS OFTEN AS YOU CAN!

This classic Thai soup really explodes with flavor. The lime leaves, sometimes called "kaffir", come from the wild lime tree, different to the limes we use in the West. The fruit tastes bitter and has a rough finish, so is discarded, and only the leaves are used. They are incredibly fragrant — spicy and lemony — and in Thailand they use them a little like we use bay leaves, to flavor soups and sauces.

THAI MUSHROOM AND COCONUT SOUP

123 calories | 10.6g fat | 9.1g saturates | 1.6g sugar | 0.3g salt | 3.8g protein | 1.5g fiber

Serves 4

14 fl oz light coconut milk

2½ cups vegetable bouillon

4 dried Kaffir lime leaves

2 lemongrass stalks, outer layers removed, core finely chopped

14 oz oyster mushrooms

2-inch piece of fresh ginger, julienned

1 teaspoon Paleo-friendly fish sauce, such as Red Boat

2 tablespoons lime juice

2 red chilies, finely chopped

a handful of fresh cilantro, chopped, to serve

In a large saucepan, mix the coconut milk, bouillon, lime leaves, and lemongrass, and bring to a boil over medium heat.

Add the mushrooms, and cook for 5 minutes, then add the ginger, fish sauce, lime juice, and chilies. Stir, and take off the heat.

Ladle the soup into serving bowls and scatter with fresh cilantro.

TIP OPT FOR THE "LIGHT" VERSION OF COCONUT MILK, AS IT REDUCES THE FAT CONTENT QUITE CONSIDERABLY, AND SACRIFICES NONE OF THE TASTE.

You often see salmon skin on the menu in Japanese restaurants, and in my opinion, it is far too good a thing to throw away — it crisps up in a pan, and adds a wonderful crunch to a salad.

SALMON AND
SALMON SKIN SALAD

633 calories | 53.2g fat | 9.6g saturates | 1.3g sugar | 0.5g salt | 36.1g protein | 3.9g fiber

Serves 4

3 x 8 oz salmon fillets, skin on
freshly ground black pepper
1 tablespoon olive oil
5 oz mixed salad leaves
2 ripe avocados, sliced

for the dressing
juice of 2 lemons
1 tablespoon Dijon mustard
6 tablespoons olive oil

Using a sharp knife, separate the salmon from the skin, and reserve for later. Cut the skin into strips about 1 inch wide, and slice each salmon fillet into four. Season both with black pepper.

Place a large nonstick pan over medium heat, and fry the salmon for 3 minutes on each side (salmon is an oily fish, so you shouldn't need to add any extra oil to the pan). Set aside to cool.

In a separate frying pan, heat the olive oil and fry the skin over high heat for about 4 minutes, or until nicely brown.

Mix all the dressing ingredients together, and dress the salad leaves and avocado slices in a large bowl. Add the salmon and salmon skin, and toss to combine.

TIP SALMON SKIN IS FATTY, BUT IT'S GOOD FAT, SO FULL OF OMEGA-3 FATTY ACIDS NECESSARY FOR HEALTHY BRAIN FUNCTION. OMEGA-3 ALSO HELPS REDUCE INFLAMMATION, AND LOWERS THE RISK OF CHRONIC DISEASES SUCH AS HEART DISEASE, CANCER, AND ARTHRITIS.

I tasted my first sashimi salad about 10 years ago, when I was in Hong Kong at Tokyo Joe's, and I instantly loved it. These days, you see it on a lot of restaurant menus, but this version is a nice, simple one you can make at home.

SEAWEED AND SASHIMI
SALAD

565 calories | 45.2g fat | 8.1g saturates | 2.3g sugar | 0.2g salt | 36.6g protein | 4.6g fiber

Serves 4

5 oz mixed salad leaves
   (including arugula)
1 avocado, chopped
4 sheets of seaweed
   paper (nori), shredded
12 cherry tomatoes,
   halved
1 tablespoon olive oil
3 tablespoons sesame
   seeds
10½ oz tuna steak
   (sashimi grade; ask
   the fish counter),
10½ oz skinless salmon
   fillet

for the dressing
4 tablespoons sesame oil
juice of 1 lemon
1 teaspoon wasabi paste
2 tablespoons olive oil

Place the salad leaves in a bowl with the avocado, shredded seaweed and tomatoes.

Heat the olive oil in a heavy nonstick griddle pan. Meanwhile, spread 1 tablespoon of the sesame seeds over a small plate, and press the tuna steak into the seeds on all sides to coat. Sear the tuna in the hot pan for 30 seconds on each side. Transfer to a chopping board, and with a sharp knife, slice thinly. Repeat the process, this time using the salmon.

Mix all the ingredients for the dressing, and toss into the salad. Add the tuna and salmon, and scatter with the remaining sesame seeds.

TIP SEAWEED IS AN EXCELLENT INGREDIENT FOR CRUMBLING INTO SOUPS, SALADS, STEWS, AND STIR FRIES. IT'S FULL OF NUTRIENTS AND VERY LOW IN CALORIES.

Seafood salad is a staple in Italian cuisine. They lightly poach incredibly fresh fish and seafood, and then pour over a great-quality olive oil to preserve it. The result melts in your mouth, and makes perfect picnic food on a hot summer's day.

ITALIAN SEAFOOD
SALAD

303 calories | 19.9g fat | 3g saturates | 2.1g sugar | 0.8g salt | 25.6g protein | 1.1g fiber

Serves 4

8 oz scallops

4 oz medium shrimp, shell on

8 oz mussels

4 oz cleaned squid, cut into rings

12 pitted Kalamata olives

6 tablespoons lemon juice

6 tablespoons olive oil

1 large garlic clove, finely chopped

1 tablespoon finely chopped flat-leaf parsley

1 tablespoon finely chopped chives

¼ teaspoon red pepper flakes

1 lemon, sliced

1 medium red onion, thinly sliced

freshly ground black pepper

Bring a large pot of water to a boil. Add the scallops, shrimp, mussels, and squid (calamari) to the boiling water, and simmer for 2 minutes, or until the seafood is cooked and the mussel shells open. Drain.

Peel the shrimp, and remove the meat from the mussel shells. Discard any mussels that remain closed.

Place the seafood in a bowl, and add all the remaining ingredients, tossing well. Chill for 30 minutes and serve.

VARIATION YOU COULD ALSO GIVE THIS DISH AN ASIAN TWIST BY USING FRESH CILANTRO, SESAME SEEDS, AND SESAME OIL.

Shrimp and avocado make a classic combination and this dressing adds an interesting new angle — fresh and citrusy.

JUMBO SHRIMP
WITH AVOCADO

404 calories | 20g fat | 3.6g saturates | 1.5g sugar | 0.9g salt | 33.9g protein | 3.9g fiber

Serves 4

1 tablespoon olive oil
1¼ lb jumbo shrimp, peeled
6 oz mixed salad leaves
2 ripe avocados, peeled, pitted, and finely chopped
freshly ground black pepper

for the dressing

juice of 1 orange
4 tablespoons olive oil
1 tablespoon lemon juice
1 tablespoon shredded basil
1 teaspoon Dijon mustard

Heat the olive oil in a large, nonstick frying pan, and fry the shrimp for 1–2 minutes on each side or until cooked through. Take off the heat and set aside.

Place the salad leaves in a large mixing bowl, and add the avocado.

In a small bowl, mix all the dressing ingredients, then toss into the salad.

Serve the salad topped with the shrimp and a grind or two of black pepper.

TIP SHRIMP ARE HIGH IN NUTRIENTS AND PROTEIN, AND LOW IN CALORIES AND FAT   PERFECT FOR WEIGHT LOSS!

I am not always a fan of sweet and sour, but this combination works very well. Try to get strawberries that are a little on the firm side, as this keeps them from being oversweet.

STRAWBERRY AND SALMON
SALAD WITH MIXED NUTS

623 calories | 48.6g fat | 7.3g saturates | 4.5g sugar | 0.3g salt | 38.8g protein | 1.9g fiber

Serves 4

1¼ lb skinless salmon
   fillets
12 large strawberries,
   thinly sliced
⅔ cup cashews, chopped
⅔ cup almonds, chopped
6 oz mixed salad leaves
your choice of fresh
   chopped herbs, such as
   chives or mint

for the dressing

4 tablespoons olive oil
juice of ½ lemon
1 tablespoon finely
   chopped chives
1 teaspoon Dijon
   mustard

Heat a dry, nonstick frying pan to high heat, and add the salmon fillets. Cook for 2–3 minutes on each side, then turn the heat down to medium, and cook for an additional 2–3 minutes. The salmon should release enough oil to cook the fish perfectly. Take off the heat and set aside.

Whisk together the dressing ingredients and set aside. Combine the strawberries with the nuts and salad leaves in a large mixing bowl.

Arrange the salad on a plate, and top with the salmon, flaked into small pieces. Dress with the vinaigrette and a scattering of fresh herbs.

TIP THERE'S NO DAIRY ON THE PALEO PLAN, BUT THERE'S NO NEED TO WORRY ABOUT YOUR CALCIUM INTAKE FOR HEALTHY BONES — ALMONDS ARE VERY CALCIUM-RICH, PLUS THEY ARE FULL OF VITAMIN E, WHICH IS GOOD FOR YOUR SKIN.

The fresh orange and cilantro, and beautiful, jewel-like pomegranate seeds make this salad a perfect winter pick-me-up — plus it's high in vitamin C to ward off any coughs and sneezes.

CHICKEN, ORANGE, AND POMEGRANATE SALAD

364 calories | 15.6g fat | 2.4g saturates | 18.1g sugar | 0.3g salt | 38.3g protein | 5.7g fiber

Serves 4

4 large oranges, peeled
  and thinly sliced
5 tablespoons olive oil
juice of ¼ lemon
a handful of cilantro,
  chopped
1 cup pomegranate seeds
  (from 1 large
  pomegranate)
4 skinless chicken
  breasts, cut into strips
freshly ground black
  pepper

Place the orange slices in a large mixing bowl. Add 3 tablespoons of the olive oil, plus the lemon juice, cilantro, and pomegranate seeds. Toss well to combine, and set aside to marinate while you cook the chicken.

Heat the remaining olive oil in a nonstick griddle pan, and sear the chicken over high heat for about 3 minutes on each side, or until cooked through. Turn off the heat, and set aside to rest for a few minutes.

To serve, divide the salad between four serving plates, top with the warm chicken slices, and finish with a few grinds of black pepper.

TIP I LOVE POMEGRANATE SEEDS. THEY'RE JUICY AND BURSTING WITH HEALTH BENEFITS — VITAMINS A, B, AND C, FOLIC ACID, FIBER, POTASSIUM, AND CALCIUM.

This meal originated in Nice, France, hence the name, but is now served all around the world. It's nicely versatile, as you can make it with fresh tuna or canned tuna, and quail's eggs or hen's eggs. It's always a winner, either way.

SALAD

NIÇOISE

514 calories | 35.9g fat | 6.8g saturates | 1g sugar | 2.3g salt | 47.3g protein | 0.8g fiber

Serves 4

4 eggs
6 oz mixed salad
  leaves or 2 romaine
  lettuces, trimmed
1 tablespoon olive oil
2 x 10½ oz tuna steaks
12–16 Kalamata olives
2 oz canned anchovies,
  drained

for the dressing
juice of 1 lemon
6 tablespoons olive oil
1 tablespoon Dijon
  mustard
1 tablespoon finely
  chopped tarragon

Place the eggs in a saucepan of boiling water, and boil for 6–7 minutes. Drain and peel. Quarter the eggs and set aside.

Whisk together the dressing ingredients in a small bowl. Place the salad leaves in a large mixing bowl, pour over the dressing, and toss well.

Heat the olive oil in a large, nonstick pan over medium heat, and sear the tuna steaks for 1–2 minutes on each side. Take out of the pan and place on a cutting board. Slice thinly.

Divide the salad between four bowls, and top with the olives, anchovies, eggs, and tuna slices.

TIP FRESH TARRAGON IS A LOVELY ADDITION TO THIS SALAD (PLUS IT PACKS A HEALTHY ANTIOXIDANT PUNCH). FILL YOUR FRIDGE WITH BUNCHES OF FRESH HERBS, AS THEY ADD INTEREST AND FLAVOR TO ANY KIND OF SALAD.

This is the simplest of salads to rustle up at a moment's notice. Quail's eggs always add a bit of class, so I often serve this as a dinner party appetizer.

QUAIL'S EGG AND PROSCIUTTO SALAD

349 calories | 28.5g fat | 5.5 g saturates | 3.5g sugar | 2g salt | 21g protein | 2.4g fiber

Serves 4

1 teaspoon olive oil
12 quail's eggs
8 oz mixed salad leaves
12 slices of Prosciutto
freshly ground black
  pepper

for the dressing
4 tablespoons walnut oil
juice of ½ lemon
1 teaspoon Dijon
  mustard

Heat a nonstick frying pan on medium heat, and add the olive oil. Crack the quail's eggs, two at a time, into the pan, and fry them as you would a normal fried egg — they only take 20–30 seconds to cook. Remove with a slotted spoon, and set aside to cool.

In a small bowl, whisk all the dressing ingredients together. Place the salad leaves in a large salad bowl, and toss with the dressing.

Arrange the salad leaves on a plate, and top with the Prosciutto and fried quail's eggs, and a grind or two of black pepper.

TIP PROSCIUTTO IS SO FULL OF FLAVOR THAT YOU DON'T NEED TO USE MUCH. TWO OR THREE WAFER-THIN SLICES ARE QUITE SUFFICIENT, AND IF YOU CUT OFF THE RIND, YOU KEEP THE FAT CONTENT NICE AND LOW.

This Thai beef salad can be served hot or cold. In Thailand, they really spice it up with lots of bird's eye chilies (one of the hottest kinds). However, if you discard the seeds, you take out a lot of the heat.

THAI BEEF
SALAD

258 calories | 9.6g fat | 3.4g saturates | 6.2g sugar | 0.3g salt | 36g protein | 1.1g fiber

Serves 4

2 x 10½ oz lean sirloin
   steaks
1 tablespoon olive oil
   (if frying)
a handful of cilantro,
   chopped, plus extra
   to garnish
a handful of mint leaves,
   chopped
2–3 bird's eye chilies,
   finely chopped
1 garlic clove, crushed
juice of 1 lemon
1-inch piece of fresh
   ginger, grated
1 tablespoon honey
8 radishes, thinly sliced
½ cucumber, thinly sliced
1 red onion, thinly sliced
freshly ground black
   pepper

Either broil the steak or fry in the olive oil for 2–3 minutes on each side until nicely browned but still a little pink in the center. Transfer to a warmed plate, and rest for 5 minutes.

In a large bowl, mix together the herbs, chilies, garlic, lemon juice, ginger, and honey.

Using a sharp knife, slice the beef into thin strips, and add them to the bowl with the dressing. Set aside to marinate while you prepare the salad.

Arrange the radish, cucumber, and red onion on a large serving platter, then top with the beef, and spoon over the marinade. Season with black pepper, and garnish with a little extra cilantro.

TIP GINGER IS A WONDER SPICE THAT STIMULATES THE APPETITE, AIDS DIGESTION, AND HELPS FIGHT OFF COLDS AND FLU.

This salad has wonderful texture — the crispy coated eggplant
that turns soft in the middle, combined with the hard crunch of the chopped
almonds. It makes a perfect lunch or light dinner.

FRIED EGGPLANT
SALAD

450 calories | 39.9g fat | 4.9g saturates | 8.5g sugar | 0.2g salt | 13.1g protein | 6.3g fiber

Serves 4

2 eggs
4 tablespoons almond
  flour
2–3 tablespoons olive oil
1 large eggplant, sliced
6 oz mixed salad leaves
2 carrots, peeled and
  grated
12 cherry tomatoes,
  halved

for the dressing
⅔ cup toasted almonds,
  roughly chopped
4 tablespoons almond oil
  or olive oil
juice of 1 lemon
a handful of fresh chives,
  chopped, plus extra
  to garnish
1 teaspoon English
  mustard powder

Whisk the eggs in a bowl, and place the almond flour on a plate.
Heat the oil in a large, nonstick frying pan over medium heat.
Dip the eggplant slices in the egg, and then in the flour, coating well.

With a slotted spoon, lower the eggplant into the hot oil, and fry for
3–4 minutes on each side. You may want to do this in a few batches.
When you put too much food in a pan, it creates moisture and poaches
the food, so do 3–4 slices at a time so you get a good color on them.

Drain on paper towels, and continue to work through the rest in
batches.

Mix all the salad dressing ingredients together, and dress the salad
leaves in a large mixing bowl. Toss in the carrots and tomatoes.

Arrange the leaves on a plate, top with the fried eggplant, and decorate
with a few chives.

VARIATION ALTERNATIVELY, FRY THE EGGPLANT FOR JUST 1 MINUTE
ON EACH SIDE AND THEN ROAST IN THE OVEN AT 400°F FOR 20
MINUTES.

Beets are a star vegetable — a great source of fiber,
excellent for detox, and full of potassium and vitamins B and C.

BEET, JICAMA, AND CARROT SALAD

333 calories | 23.4g fat | 3.3g saturates | 18.1g sugar | 0.3g salt | 7.9g protein | 9.4g fiber

Serves 4

juice of ½ orange
juice of ½ lemon
4 tablespoons olive oil
10½ oz carrots, grated
14 oz beets, grated
10½ oz jicama, grated
freshly ground black
　pepper
¾ cup sunflower seeds
chopped fresh cilantro

In a small bowl, mix together the orange juice, lemon juice, and olive oil.

In a large bowl, mix together the carrot, beets, and jicama. Pour over the dressing, season with pepper, and toss well.

Serve the salad on a plate with a scattering of sunflower seeds, and some chopped fresh cilantro.

TIP JICAMA IS A SWEET ROOT VEGETABLE THAT LOOKS LIKE A TURNIP. IT'S OFTEN USED IN SOUTH AMERICAN AND ASIAN COOKING, AND PACKS A HEALTHY PUNCH — RICH IN FIBER, LIKE BEETS, AND HIGH IN VITAMIN C.

TOMATO, CAPER, AND RED ONION SALAD

59 calories | 3.2g fat | 0.5g saturates | 6.2g sugar | trace salt | 1.2g protein | 2.2g fiber

Serves 4

4 large tomatoes, sliced
¼ red onion, sliced
1 tablespoon capers
1 tablespoon olive oil
1 tablespoon balsamic
　vinegar

Arrange the tomatoes, red onion, and capers on a plate, and drizzle with the olive oil and balsamic vinegar.

TIP CAPERS ADD INTEREST TO ANY SALAD, AND PACK A MIGHTY ANTIOXIDANT PUNCH. THEY'RE ALSO GREAT WITH MANY FISH DISHES AND SAUCES.

Mirin is alcoholic, so on the "consume in moderation" list for Paleo. However, it is so delicious with grated carrot — enhancing its natural sweetness — that I had to include it for a one-off treat.

SESAME CARROT SALAD

95 calories | 6.1g fat | 1.1g saturates | 6.7g sugar | 0.1g salt | 2.4g protein | 3.9g fiber

Serves 4

1¾ lb carrots, peeled
6–8 tablespoons sesame seeds
2 tablespoons mirin (rice wine)

Coarsely grate the carrots, and place in a large bowl.

In a mortar and pestle, grind the sesame seeds to a paste, add the mirin, and mix well.

Pour the mirin dressing over the carrots, toss well, and serve.

Arugula leaves are my favorite salad leaves, as they have a punchy, peppery flavor that does not need to be dressed in copious amounts of olive oil. I also love to add this as an extra topping to my pesto pizza (see page 68).

ARUGULA SALAD

240 calories | 22.7g fat | 2.9g saturates | 5.7g sugar | 0.3g salt | 2.9g protein | 2.7g fiber

Serves 4

8 oz arugula leaves
1 red onion, finely sliced
20 cherry tomatoes, halved
freshly ground black pepper

for the dressing
juice of 1 lemon
6 tablespoons olive oil
1 tablespoon Dijon mustard
2 tablespoons pine nuts
½ garlic clove
6–8 fresh basil leaves

Place all the salad ingredients in a large mixing bowl and toss to combine.

Place all the dressing ingredients in a food processor or blender, and blitz until smooth. Pour over the salad, season with black pepper, toss well, and serve.

Papaya is the fruit of the papaw tree, and in Asia, is known to help digestion. For this very traditional Thai salad, the trick is to use the under-ripe fruit (green rather than orange), as this gives the salad a wonderful crunch, and is the perfect way to eat it.

THAI GREEN PAPAYA SALAD

176 calories | 7.7g fat | 1.6g saturates | 16.8g sugar | 2.3g salt | 8.1g protein | 3g fiber

Serves 4

1 green papaya, grated
12 cherry tomatoes, halved
4 tablespoons chopped cashew nuts
2 tablespoons dried shrimp
freshly ground black pepper
a handful of cilantro, chopped

for the dressing

3 garlic cloves, crushed
1 small red chili, finely chopped
2 tablespoons lemon juice
2 tablespoons Red Boat fish sauce
2 tablespoons raw honey

Place all the salad ingredients except the cilantro in a large bowl, and toss to combine.

In a small bowl, combine all the dressing ingredients and whisk. Pour the dressing over the salad, and toss again. Season with black pepper, scatter with fresh cilantro and serve.

TIP THE TRADITIONAL THAI DISH HAS PEANUTS AND PALM SUGAR, WHICH I HAVE SWAPPED FOR CASHEWS AND HONEY INSTEAD, TO MAKE IT SUITABLE FOR THE PALEO PLAN.

Potatoes contain potentially harmful antinutrients, and are therefore not included on the Paleo plan, but butternut squash is the perfect vegetable replacement to satisfy all your carb cravings.

BUTTERNUT SQUASH AND PUMPKIN SEED SALAD

433 calories | 30.8g fat | 4.5g saturates | 15.7g sugar | 0.1g salt | 10.6g protein | 8.1g fiber

Serves 4

1 large butternut squash, peeled and cut in half (seeds discarded)
2 tablespoons olive oil
1 tablespoon chopped thyme
1 tablespoon raw honey, melted
8 oz arugula leaves
1 scant cup toasted pumpkin seeds
freshly ground black pepper

for the dressing

4 tablespoons olive oil
juice of ½ lemon
juice of ½ orange
1 teaspoon Dijon mustard
1 teaspoon chopped thyme leaves

Preheat the oven to 425°F.

Chop the butternut squash into wedges, and place in a large bowl. Drizzle over the oil, add the thyme, and toss to coat. Place on a baking sheet, and cook in the oven for 30 minutes. Every 10 minutes, remove the baking sheet, and toss the squash so that all the edges become roasted and caramelized. After 30 minutes, toss one last time, drizzle with the honey, cook for an additional 5 minutes, then set aside to cool slightly.

Meanwhile, mix all the dressing ingredients together, and dress the arugula leaves in a large bowl. Scatter the pumpkin seeds on top and toss with the butternut squash. Finish with a few grinds of black pepper and serve.

TIP BUTTERNUT SQUASH HAS A LOVELY SWEET, NUTTY TASTE, SO YOU DON'T HAVE TO DO MUCH TO IT. I LOVE TO EAT IT RAW, BUT IT'S REALLY PERFECT ROASTED, WHEN IT CARAMELIZES BEAUTIFULLY.

This very simple salad never fails to impress. Figs have a lovely delicate flavor, and taste fantastic when they are broiled. Here, the honey brings out all their natural sweetness, while the truffle oil adds a contrasting rich earthiness — you must try it!

ROASTED FIGS IN TRUFFLE OIL AND HONEY

171 calories | 8.8g fat | 1.3g saturates | 22.3g sugar | 0.3g salt | 1.6g protein | 2g fiber

Serves 4

12 ripe figs, cut in half
3 tablespoons white
   truffle oil
3 tablespoons raw honey,
   melted
3 tablespoons chopped
   basil
5 oz arugula leaves

for the vinaigrette
1 tablespoon Dijon
   mustard
1 tablespoon raw honey,
   melted
juice of 1 lemon
olive oil, to taste
   (optional)

Preheat the broiler to high.

Arrange the figs on a baking sheet, cut-side up.

Whisk together the truffle oil, honey, and basil in a small bowl, and pour this dressing over the figs, reserving a little for later.

Place the figs under the broiler and cook for 3–5 minutes, until the sauce starts to bubble up and the figs caramelize.

Pour off the cooking juices into the bowl with the reserved truffle dressing, and whisk in the ingredients for the vinaigrette.

Serve the figs on a bed of arugula leaves, dressed with the honey-mustard vinaigrette.

TIP FIGS CONTAIN MORE FIBER THAN ALMOST ANY OTHER FRUIT OR VEGETABLE. THIS IS A REAL BENEFIT WHEN YOU'RE ON A DIET, AS THEIR SLOW-RELEASE ENERGY WILL KEEP YOU FEELING FULL FOR LONGER.

MAIN MEALS

This is one of my favorite meals, as it immediately conjures up images of sitting in a Parisian café with a crisp green salad and a glass of (non-Paleo) red wine.

CLASSIC STEAK
TARTARE

524 calories | 38.4g fat | 15.1g saturates | 2.1g sugar | 1g salt | 41.7g protein | 0.9g fiber

Serves 4

1 white onion, finely chopped
2 tablespoons finely chopped flat-leaf parsley
2 egg yolks, beaten
1¾ lb lean ground beef
a dash of Tabasco sauce
1 tablespoon Dijon mustard
1 tablespoon roughly chopped capers
1 garlic clove, finely chopped
1 tablespoon olive oil
freshly ground black pepper
3½ oz salad leaves

Mix all the ingredients except the salad leaves in a large bowl, and season with black pepper.

Cover the bowl, and chill in the fridge for 30 minutes.

Arrange the steak mix on individual plates (use a ring if you want consistent shapes). Serve with a crisp green salad.

TIP MAKE SURE THE BEEF YOU BUY IS VERY FRESH AND LEAN. GRASS-FED IS BEST FOR THE PALEO PLAN.

VARIATION USE WHITE TRUFFLE OIL IN PLACE OF THE OLIVE OIL FOR A RICHER FLAVOR.

This dish is so healthy — tuna is a fish with very little to
no fat content, and the lemon is chock-full of vitamin C.

SEARED LEMON TUNA
WITH OLIVE TAPENADE

421 calories | 27.9g fat | 4.9g saturates | 0.6g sugar | 1.6g salt | 41.9g protein | 2.8g fiber

Serves 4

4–6 tablespoons extra-
virgin olive oil
4 x 6-oz tuna steaks
juice of 3 lemons
a handful of fresh chives,
finely chopped
a few basil leaves,
shredded
freshly ground black
pepper
5 oz arugula leaves

for the tapenade

7 oz pitted black olives
1 tablespoon capers
1 tablespoon chopped
tarragon
1 garlic clove, peeled
3–5 anchovy fillets
juice of ½ lemon

Either in a food processor or with a sharp knife, finely chop all
the tapenade ingredients, except the lemon juice, to a coarse paste.
Transfer to a bowl, add the lemon juice and stir to combine.

Heat 1 tablespoon of the olive oil in a griddle pan over medium-high
heat, and sear the tuna steaks for 2 minutes on each side. Add the
lemon juice, then take off the heat, add the remaining olive oil, and
swirl the pan to mix.

Serve the tuna on a plate, drizzle over the lemony oil, and scatter
the chives on top. Finish with a spoonful of tapenade, a scattering
of shredded basil leaves and a few grinds of black pepper. Serve with
a side of fresh arugula leaves.

TIP IF YOU OVERCOOK FRESH TUNA, IT BECOMES THE SAME
AS CANNED, SO MAKE SURE IT IS NICE AND RARE ON THE INSIDE.

Salmon is considered by many to be one of the healthiest foods you can eat — some say the healthiest. It is rich in heart-healthy omega-3 fatty acids, and reduces the risk of numerous cardiovascular problems.

HERBED SALMON
WITH LEMON DRESSING

485 calories | 36.5g fat | 5.8g saturates | 1g sugar | 0.5g salt | 37.8g protein | 1.7g fiber

Serves 4

4 x 6-oz skinless salmon
  fillets
a handful of fresh basil
a handful of fresh
  flat-leaf parsley
a handful of fresh
  tarragon
a handful of fresh chives
a handful of fresh
  cilantro
1 head of broccoli, broken
  into florets

for the dressing
6 tablespoons olive oil
1 tablespoon Dijon
  mustard
3 tablespoons lemon juice

Place the skinless salmon fillets in a large sauté pan and cover with water. Set on the stove, bring the water to a boil, and then immediately remove from the heat. Cover the pan with a lid, and let stand for 15 minutes while the salmon gently poaches.

Next, make the dressing. Mix all the dressing ingredients together in a small bowl, and set aside.

Heap all your herbs together on a chopping board and chop until fine (a mezzaluna is perfect for this).

Set a steamer or colander over a pan of boiling water, and steam the broccoli, covered, for 4–5 minutes.

Take the salmon, one fillet at a time, and roll in the herbs so that it is coated on all sides.

Arrange the salmon on a plate, and drizzle over the citrusy dressing. Serve with the steamed broccoli.

TIP SALMON IS A LEAN PROTEIN THAT IS DIGESTED SLOWLY, SO IT KEEPS YOU FEELING FULL LONG AFTER A MEAL. ENJOY A NICE BIG PORTION.

When I first came up with this recipe, I used wasabi peas, but as these are not part of the Paleo plan, I had to look around for a substitute. The macadamia nuts were the perfect solution. This is one of the best dishes I have made.

WASABI CRUSTED HALIBUT ON BOK CHOY

673 calories | 37.4g fat | 5.6g saturates | 1.4g sugar | 0.7g salt | 82.4g protein | 3.4g fiber

Serves 4

2 tablespoons almond flour
2 tablespoons sesame seeds
1 tablespoon sesame oil, plus extra to drizzle
⅔ cup macadamia nuts
2 teaspoons wasabi powder or paste
1 egg
4 large bok choy
4 x 8-oz halibut fillets
1 tablespoon olive oil
1 lime, quartered
freshly ground black pepper
a handful of fresh cilantro, chopped

Place the almond flour, sesame seeds, sesame oil, macadamia nuts, wasabi, and egg in a food processor and blend until smooth.

Bring a saucepan of water to a boil, and steam the bok choy for 5 minutes. Drain, and then plunge the leaves into a bowl of ice water to stop the cooking process, and keep them green.

Transfer the wasabi mix to a shallow dish, and press the halibut fillets into the mixture so they are thoroughly coated on both sides.

Heat the oil in a heavy, nonstick sauté pan, and sear the halibut for 2–3 minutes on each side.

Serve the halibut over the bok choy, and drizzle with a little sesame oil. Add a squeeze of lime, a twist of pepper, and a scattering of cilantro.

TIP THIS DISH IS ALSO LOVELY WITH OTHER TYPES OF FISH, AND I PARTICULARLY RECOMMEND BOTH COD AND TUNA.

Sesame with tuna is one of those classic flavor combinations that just works, and adding a little coconut to the mix sweetens it up very deliciously.

SESAME AND COCONUT CRUSTED TUNA

567 calories | 29.1g fat | 8g saturates | 1g sugar | 0.5g salt | 67.8g protein | 7g fiber

Serves 4

2 tablespoons coconut flour
3 tablespoons sesame seeds
a handful of fresh cilantro
1 garlic clove, peeled
2 eggs
4 x 9–10-oz tuna steaks
2 tablespoons olive oil
arugula salad (see page 110)

Place the coconut flour, sesame seeds, cilantro, and garlic in a blender or food processor and blitz to a fine grain. Tip this onto a large plate, and spread out in a thin layer. Crack the eggs into a bowl and whisk lightly together.

Dip the tuna steaks in the egg, and then in the coconut and sesame seed mixture, so they are coated on all sides.

Heat 1 tablespoon of the oil in a large, nonstick frying pan, and sear the tuna steaks (two at a time) for 1–2 minutes on each side, until the coating has turned golden brown.

Take out of the pan, and set aside while you cook the other tuna steaks in the remaining oil.

Slice the tuna into thin strips, and serve with the arugula salad.

It is important to keep the shrimp heads on for this recipe, as they deliciously flavor the sauce.

PEEL-AND-EAT
SHRIMP

289 calories | 12.5g fat | 1.8g saturates | 0g sugar | 1.2g salt | 44g protein | 0g fiber

Serves 4

4 tablespoons olive oil
2¼ lb large, unpeeled
    heads-on shrimp,
    deveined
3 garlic cloves, crushed
1 teaspoon chili powder
juice of 1 lemon
a handful of fresh basil
    leaves, thinly shredded

Heat the olive oil in a large saucepan over medium heat, and add the shrimp, garlic, chili powder, and lemon juice. Cover and cook for 4–5 minutes.

Add the shredded basil to the saucepan, and toss to mix. Remove the shrimp from the pan, divide between four bowls, and serve with the cooking juice for dipping.

VARIATION IF YOU WOULD LIKE TO SPICE UP THE SAUCE EVEN MORE, ADD A FINELY CHOPPED BIRD'S EYE CHILI.

TIP THIS IS A CHEF'S TRICK FOR SHREDDING BASIL LEAVES INCREDIBLY THINLY — ROLL EACH LEAF UP LIKE A CIGAR AND THEN SLICE THINLY. VOILA!

This dish has everything we love about deep-fried food — just without the guilt. Make an extra-large batch, as you'll be amazed how quickly it all goes.

COCONUT SHRIMP
WITH BROCCOLI

406 calories | 31.1g fat | 7.4g saturates | 3g sugar | 0.5g salt | 22.1g protein | 8.4g fiber

Serves 4

14 oz broccoli florets
2 tablespoons almond oil
  or olive oil
2 tablespoons almond
  flakes
10½ oz peeled large
  shrimp
3 tablespoons coconut
  flour
freshly ground black
  pepper
4 tablespoons olive oil
1 lemon or lime, cut into
  wedges
a handful of cilantro,
  chopped

for the dipping sauce

6–8 tablespoons light
  coconut milk
1 tablespoon sesame oil
1 tablespoon sesame
  seeds

Bring a saucepan of water to a simmer over medium heat, and cook the broccoli for 3–4 minutes. Drain, and plunge into a bowl of ice water to prevent the florets from cooking any more in their own steam.

Transfer the broccoli to a mixing bowl, and toss it in the almond oil and almond flakes.

Put the shrimp and coconut flour into a ziplock bag, season with black pepper, and shake to coat thoroughly.

To make the dipping sauce, combine all the ingredients in a small saucepan, and stir over low heat. Bring to a simmer, and pour into a serving dish.

In a large, nonstick sauté pan, heat the olive oil over low heat. Add the shrimp, and cook for about 2 minutes on each side, taking care that they don't burn.

Arrange the shrimp and broccoli on a plate, squeeze over the lemon or lime juice, and scatter with some cilantro. Serve the dipping sauce separately on the side.

TIP LIGHTLY BATTER THE SHRIMP, AS YOU ONLY NEED A DUSTING OF THE FLOUR TO GET THE BEST OUT OF THIS DISH.

This Italian-inspired dish is all I want to eat when I'm dining al fresco — perfect for a summer lunch in the garden or a dinner under the stars. The salsa verde is fantastic with any fish or seafood, and also works well with chicken.

MIXED GRILL
WITH SALSA VERDE

667 calories | 43g fat | 7.3g saturates | 3g sugar | 1.5g salt | 66.4g protein | 4.5g fiber

Serves 6

2 x 7 oz swordfish
   steaks, cut in half
2 x 7 oz salmon steaks,
   cut in half
2 x 7 oz tuna steaks,
   cut in half
2 tablespoons olive oil
freshly ground black
   pepper
1 lemon, cut into wedges

for the salsa verde
1 tablespoon capers
6 tablespoons olive oil
6–8 fresh basil leaves
1 teaspoon Dijon
   mustard
juice of 1 lemon
1 tablespoon chopped
   tarragon
3 tablespoons finely
   chopped shallots

Preheat a griddle pan, and brush the fish with 1 tablespoon of the olive oil. Sear the fish in the hot pan for 2–3 minutes on each side. Set aside.

Meanwhile, place all the salsa verde ingredients, except the shallots, in a food processor, and blitz until they are finely chopped — you want to keep a little texture, so be careful not to purée them. Transfer to a bowl, and stir in the shallots.

Serve the fish with the salsa verde on the side. Finish with a few grinds of black pepper, and a squeeze of fresh lemon. This is delicious with a tomato and red onion salad.

I love this dish hot and spicy, so add more chili if you like. Make sure you don't go over on these cooking times, as the squid should be succulent and tender, not rubbery and chewy.

STUFFED SQUID
WITH TOMATO SAUCE

412 calories | 16.4g fat | 3.1g saturates | 4.5g sugar | 1.6g salt | 58.3g protein | 1.4g fiber

Serves 4

8 small squid
10½ oz cooked skinless salmon fillet
7 oz cooked, peeled shrimp
2 garlic cloves, peeled
2 tablespoons sun-dried tomato paste
1 egg
a handful of fresh basil, chopped, plus extra to garnish
freshly ground black pepper
1 tablespoon olive oil

for the tomato sauce

1 tablespoon olive oil
½ red onion, finely chopped
14 oz canned chopped tomatoes
1 garlic clove, crushed
1 small bird's eye chili, finely chopped
¼ cup vegetable bouillon

First prepare the squid. Remove the tentacles and reserve. Pull away the wings, remove the head, and empty the main tube of cartilage and slime. Pull or cut away the eyes and beak, and remove anything else that feels hard or slimy from the tentacles. Discard everything but the cleaned tentacles and main body tube. Wash well and dry.

To make the stuffing, place the salmon, shrimp, peeled whole garlic cloves, sun-dried tomato paste, egg, and basil in a food processor and purée until smooth.

Fill each squid about two-thirds full with the stuffing and press it down. Secure the end with a cocktail stick, and set aside until ready to cook.

To make the tomato sauce, heat the oil in a wide sauté pan over medium heat, and fry the onion until soft. Add the tomatoes, crushed garlic, chili, and bouillon and heat to a low simmer, stirring to combine.

Take a nonstick griddle pan, and place over moderate heat. Season the squid with black pepper. Add 1 tablespoon oil to the pan, and add the squid. Cook for 2 minutes on one side, then turn over and cook for an additional 2 minutes.

Transfer the squid to the pan with the tomato sauce, and cook, covered, over medium to low heat for about 12–15 minutes. Turn halfway through the cooking time. Serve the squid with the tomato sauce and some basil scattered on top.

Honey and ginger are two of my favorite ingredients as they create magic when cooked together. Both are also excellent for the immune system, so this makes a lovely dinner all through the winter months.

HONEY-GLAZED SALMON WITH GINGER

707 calories | 44.2g fat | 7.4g saturates | 13.8g sugar | 0.6g salt | 63.8g protein | 4.6g fiber

Serves 4

4 x 8-oz skinless
   salmon fillets

for the glaze
2 tablespoons raw honey
1 tablespoon Dijon
   mustard
juice of 1 lemon
1-inch piece of fresh
   ginger, peeled
   and grated

for the cabbage
3 tablespoons olive oil
1 small cabbage, sliced
   into thin strips
1 garlic clove, crushed
1 tablespoon sesame
   seeds, plus extra
   to garnish
freshly ground black
   pepper
4 scallions, chopped

Heat a large, nonstick pan over high heat, and add the salmon — if you have a good-quality, nonstick pan, there should be enough oils in the salmon to cook it without the need to add any extra oil. Cook the salmon for 3–4 minutes on each side.

Meanwhile, make the glaze. Place the honey, mustard, lemon, and ginger together in a bowl and stir to combine. Set aside.

When your salmon is just about cooked, spoon the glaze over the top, then take off the heat. The glaze will caramelize in the hot pan, and turn the salmon sticky and brown.

To cook the cabbage, heat half the olive oil in a wok over medium heat. Add the cabbage and stir-fry for 3–4 minutes, then add the remaining oil, and cook for another 5 minutes, tossing all the time (if you need more moisture, add a drop or two of water). Add the garlic and sesame seeds, and cook for another minute.

Turn the cabbage out onto a plate, season with black pepper, and top with the glazed salmon. Scatter the scallions over the top, and serve with a few extra sesame seeds.

Macadamia nuts are grown in tropical countries, and are one of the more expensive nuts to purchase. However, they are full of health benefits, and taste deliciously crunchy and buttery. I highly recommend them.

SALMON WITH MACADAMIA
AND ALMOND CRUST

686 calories | 54g fat | 7g saturates | 2g sugar | 0.3g salt | 45g protein | 3g fiber

Serves 4

¾ cup unsalted almonds
½ cup macadamia nuts
2 eggs
¾ cup almond flour
2 tablespoons olive or almond oil
4 x 6 oz skinless salmon fillets
1 bunch watercress
½ lemon, cut into wedges
freshly ground black pepper

Preheat the oven to 400°F.

Place the nuts in a food processor, and give them a quick whizz. Add the eggs, almond flour, and 1 tablespoon of the oil, and blend.

Place the salmon on a baking sheet, and spread the nut mix over the top in a thick layer. Bake in the oven for 15–18 minutes.

Toss the watercress in the rest of the oil, and a squeeze of lemon, and divide between four plates. Serve the salmon on top, and season with a grind of black pepper.

Nothing beats a good Thai chicken curry, and this recipe keeps it nice and authentic. The only thing missing is a bowl of steamed jasmine rice, but when you have flavors this bold, and a sauce this creamy, it's no hardship to do without any accompaniment, and double-up on curry instead.

THAI CHICKEN

CURRY

429 calories | 19.3g fat | 10.5g saturates | 3.9g sugar | 0.8g salt | 57.8g protein | 2.8g fiber

Serves 4

2 tablespoons olive oil
1 red onion, sliced
2 lb skinless chicken breasts, sliced
1 tablespoon Thai red curry paste
14 fl oz light coconut milk
3–4 dried Kaffir lime leaves
12 oz spinach
a handful of fresh cilantro, chopped

Heat the olive oil in a large, nonstick pan, and sweat the onion for 3–5 minutes, turning constantly.

Add the chicken to the pan and cook, stirring, for 5 minutes.

Add the curry paste, and cook, stirring, for a minute, then add the coconut milk, and reduce the heat to low. Add the lime leaves and spinach, and simmer, covered, for 8 minutes.

Divide the curry between four bowls, and serve scattered with fresh cilantro.

TIP ALWAYS MAKE SURE YOU OPT FOR SKINLESS CHICKEN BREASTS WHEN YOU ARE WATCHING YOUR WEIGHT, AS THEY CONTAIN ONLY 1G SATURATED FAT PER 3½ OZ SERVING.

Chinese food is always a favorite, but it's hard to make on the Paleo diet, as you can't have traditional soy, oyster, or hoisin sauce. There are alternatives you can try, but here the ginger and cilantro provide so much flavor, that you really don't need anything else — except maybe a drizzle of sesame oil, if you like.

CHINESE WOK-FRIED CHICKEN
WITH GINGER AND HONEY

390 calories | 16.4g fat | 3g saturates | 11.6g sugar | 0.6g salt | 47.1g protein | 5.3g fiber

Serves 4

2¼ tablespoons olive oil
1-inch piece of fresh
   ginger, peeled
   and grated
2 garlic cloves, finely
   sliced
1½ lb skinless chicken
   breasts, cut into strips
freshly ground black
   pepper
4–6 baby bok choy, halved
1 tablespoon raw honey
2 red peppers, seeded
   and sliced
4 tablespoons chopped
   cilantro, plus extra
   to garnish
2 tablespoons lime juice
   (or lemon juice)
½ cup cashews, chopped,
   plus extra to garnish
5 scallions, chopped,
   plus extra to garnish

In a large, nonstick wok, heat 1 tablespoon of the oil over medium heat, and fry the ginger and garlic until lightly golden. Tip out of the pan.

In the same wok, heat 1 tablespoon of the olive oil over medium heat. Season the chicken with black pepper, and stir-fry for a few minutes on each side until brown.

Return the ginger and garlic to the pan, add the remaining olive oil, and cook the bok choy for about 4–5 minutes. Add all the remaining ingredients to the pan, tossing everything together, and stir-frying for 3–4 minutes until the stir-fry is a little golden from the honey.

Serve in a bowl with a scattering of scallions, extra cashews, and a few cilantro leaves to garnish.

TIP WHEN STIR-FRYING, DON'T BE TEMPTED TO REACH FOR THE SNOW PEAS OR SUGAR SNAP PEAS, AS THESE ARE LEGUMES, SO NOT PALEO-FRIENDLY FOODS. LEGUMES CONTAIN PHYTIC ACID, WHICH CAN OBSTRUCT THE ABSORPTION OF NUTRIENTS, AND LEAD TO DIGESTIVE PROBLEMS.

This is a lovely BBQ recipe for a hot summer's day, and also for when you want to bring the outdoors indoors, as you can cook it in the oven. The sauce is fantastic, and I always make double, so I can freeze a batch for another time (just make sure you discard any that has come into contact with raw chicken).

PERFECT BBQ
CHICKEN

250 calories | 2.7g fat | 0.7g saturates | 6.9g sugar | 0.7g salt | 49.4g protein | 1g fiber

Serves 4

4 x 7 oz skinless chicken breasts
5 oz mixed salad leaves or grilled artichokes (see page 70)

for the BBQ sauce

1 tablespoon raw honey
3 tablespoons tomato paste
1 tablespoon sun-dried tomato paste
2 garlic cloves, crushed
2 tablespoons white vinegar
1 tablespoon dried rosemary
1 tablespoon Dijon mustard

Fire up the barbecue or preheat the oven to 400°F.

First make the BBQ sauce. Melt the honey in a saucepan over low heat. Add all the remaining BBQ sauce ingredients, stir well, and take off the heat. Divide the sauce between two bowls.

Place the chicken in one of the bowls, cover with plastic wrap, and set aside in the fridge to marinate while the barbecue heats up. Cover the remaining bowl of sauce with plastic wrap, and set aside.

Grill the chicken on the barbecue for 5 minutes on each side or until cooked through. Turn regularly and, each time, brush the chicken with the marinade. (If using an oven, cook for 20 minutes, turning halfway through, and brushing with the marinade.)

Serve the chicken with a simple salad or grilled artichokes — and don't forget the second bowl of BBQ sauce for extra dipping.

TIP REMOVING THE CHICKEN SKIN LOWERS THE FAT.

Sadly, school lunches have put a lot of people off calves' liver, and it's such a shame, as when it's not overcooked and still a little pink on the inside, it's delicious — especially with a slice of bacon and a dollop of English mustard on the side.

CALVES' LIVER

WITH ROASTED LEMONS

426 calories | 24.2g fat | 4.2g saturates | 25.1g sugar | 0.3g salt | 26.2g protein | 1.4g fiber

Serves 4

3 tablespoons olive oil
2 medium red onions,
   finely sliced
2 tablespoons raw honey
freshly ground black
   pepper
20 oz calves' liver,
   thinly sliced
5 oz mixed salad leaves
   or arugula

for the lemons
12 unwaxed lemons,
   quartered
4–6 tablespoons olive oil
4 garlic cloves, crushed
4 tablespoons raw honey,
   melted

Preheat the oven to 425°F.

First prepare the lemons. Place the quarters in a roasting pan, and mix with the olive oil, garlic, and honey. Cook in the oven for 30–40 minutes, or until the lemons have turned golden brown.

Heat 2 tablespoons of the olive oil in a large sauté pan, and fry the onions for 3–5 minutes. Add the honey, turn the heat down, and cook for an additional 3 minutes on low heat, or until the onions are caramelized. Set aside.

Heat the rest of the olive oil in a large frying pan over high heat. Season the liver and sear for 1–2 minutes on each side (I like mine nice and pink in the middle, so would cook for just 1 minute). Serve with the onion and roasted lemons, and a mixed leaf salad on the side.

TIP ALTHOUGH CALVES' LIVER IS MODERATELY HIGH IN FAT, IT IS ALSO HIGH IN ZINC, IRON, AND VITAMINS B12 AND B6.

This Greek classic is my go-to recipe for Friday night dinner. It's simple to make, but tastes so satisfying that you never get bored with it, plus any leftovers make a lovely Saturday lunch, served cold with a crisp green salad.

GREEK-STYLE
LEMON CHICKEN

517 calories | 15g fat | 3g saturates | 4.7g sugar | 0.6g salt | 90.9g protein | 0.6g fiber

Serves 4

3 tablespoons olive oil
1 tablespoon raw honey, melted
juice of 1 lemon
1 teaspoon cayenne pepper
freshly ground black pepper
1 chicken (approx 5 lb), cut into 10 pieces
1 whole head of garlic, separated into unpeeled cloves
2 unwaxed lemons, cut into wedges
2 sprigs of rosemary
a handful of flat-leaf parsley, chopped
7 oz mixed salad leaves or the Greek salad on page 149

Preheat the oven to 400°F.

In a large bowl, mix the olive oil, honey, lemon juice, and cayenne pepper together. Season the chicken pieces with black pepper, add to the bowl, and massage the marinade into the skin with your hands.

Place the chicken pieces in a roasting pan, and add the garlic cloves, lemon wedges and rosemary. Mix well together, and ensure everything is well spread out. Season.

Roast in the hot oven for 40 minutes, until the chicken has turned golden brown, and the lemons have started to caramelize.

Serve this straight from the roasting pan, with a scattering of fresh parsley, and a salad on the side.

TIP LEMONS ARE ACIDIC, BUT IN FACT THEIR EFFECT ON THE BODY IS ALKALIZING, SO THEY HELP RESTORE BALANCE TO THE BODY'S PH.

Saffron is a very expensive spice, but a pinch goes a long way, and it lends a beautiful color to this roasted chicken.

ROASTED CHICKEN

WITH SAFFRON

444 calories | 9g fat | 2g saturates | 0g sugar | 1.3g salt | 90.6g protein | 0g fiber

Serves 4

1 whole chicken
  (approx. 5 lb)
1 lemon, cut into
  6 wedges
1 whole head of garlic,
  broken up
1 bouillon cube, broken
  into 4 pieces
1 tablespoon olive oil
1 teaspoon saffron
  threads
freshly ground black
  pepper

Preheat the oven to 425°F.

Stuff the cavity of the chicken with the lemon wedges, garlic cloves, and pieces of stock cube.

Place the chicken in a roasting pan, and drizzle over the olive oil. Sprinkle over the saffron threads, season with black pepper, and massage the flavorings into the skin.

Roast in the oven for approximately 2 hours, or until the juices run clear, and the bird is cooked through.

Remove from the oven, and serve with a drizzle of the cooking juices, and a side of your choice.

> **TIP** TRY AND BUY FREE-RANGE CHICKENS FROM A TRUSTED, LOCAL SOURCE AS IT'S IMPORTANT TO KNOW THEY FED ON PESTICIDE-FREE GRASS.

If you have good-quality meat and great seasonings, you can often do away with the burger bun, and not miss it at all. However, as a Paleo alternative, fry two large portobello mushrooms in a little oil and sandwich the burger between these. You can even sprinkle sesame seeds on top if you like.

BEEF
BURGERS

595 calories | 38.6g fat | 11.8g saturates | 3.9g sugar | 0.7g salt | 57.3g protein | 3.8g fiber

Serves 4

2 lb lean ground beef
1 red onion, halved
  (½ finely chopped)
2 tablespoons sun-dried
  tomato paste
2 eggs, beaten
2 garlic cloves, crushed
4 tablespoons almond
  flour
2 tablespoons olive oil
7 oz mixed salad leaves

Place the ground beef, chopped onion, sun-dried tomato paste, eggs, garlic, and almond flour in a large mixing bowl, and stir to combine. Using your hands, shape into four equal-sized patties.

Heat the olive oil in a large, nonstick pan over high heat, and cook the burgers for 3–4 minutes on each side. Reduce the heat, and cook for a few more minutes on each side, until the meat is cooked medium to well-done.

Slice the remaining onion into ¼-inch thick round slices. Top each burger with slices of onion and serve over a crunchy green salad.

TIP AS A GENERAL RULE, THE LEANER THE BEEF, THE BETTER THE BURGER.

This dish is home comfort food at its best. If you want to mix a Green and Red recipe, then this one is brilliant with the acorn squash spaghetti on page 158. The sauce is rich, so make sure you buy the leanest ground meat you can, or grind the meat yourself in a food processor.

ITALIAN

MEATBALLS

546 calories | 31.9g fat | 10.4g saturates | 10.8g sugar | 0.9g salt | 53.9g protein | 4g fiber

Serves 4

30 oz lean ground beef
½ medium onion, finely
    chopped
2 garlic cloves, crushed
2 tablespoons almond
    flour
1 egg, lightly beaten
1 tablespoon chopped
    flat-leaf parsley,
    plus extra to garnish
4 tablespoons tomato
    paste
1 tablespoon olive oil
torn basil, to garnish

for the tomato sauce

1 tablespoon olive oil
1 garlic clove, crushed
28 oz canned chopped
    tomatoes
4 tablespoons sun-dried
    tomato paste
⅔ cup vegetable bouillon

First make the meatballs. In a large mixing bowl, mix the beef, onion, garlic, almond flour, and egg, using your hands to thoroughly combine. Add the parsley, and half the tomato paste, and again, mix well. Using your hands again, roll the mixture into 20 or so balls, and set aside.

Now for the tomato sauce. Heat the olive oil in a large casserole dish or saucepan over medium heat. Once hot, add the garlic, and cook gently for a few minutes until aromatic, then add the chopped tomatoes and sun-dried tomato paste, and stir to combine.

Heat the remaining tablespoon of oil in a large casserole dish over high heat, and cook the meatballs for about 1 minute on each side, turning with a wooden spoon until they are brown all over. Add the tomato sauce, bouillon, and remaining tomato paste. Reduce the heat, and cook for 10 minutes, covered, then remove the lid and simmer for another 5 minutes to reduce the liquid.

Serve with a scattering of parsley and basil.

The sesame seeds and sesame oil lend this recipe a slightly oriental feel, but then the pine nuts and basil are a little more Italian-inspired. It's a lovely combination — you'll see!

SESAME STEAKS
ON BROCCOLI PURÉE

761 calories | 45.6g fat | 10.7g saturates | 3.3g sugar | 0.6g salt | 83.1g protein | 8.7g fiber

Serves 4

4 tablespoons sesame seeds
4 x 10-oz sirloin steaks, trimmed of fat
1¾ lb broccoli florets
4 tablespoons chopped garlic
2 tablespoons toasted pine nuts, plus extra to garnish
6–8 fresh basil leaves, torn, plus extra to garnish
6 tablespoons olive oil, plus extra for frying
freshly ground black pepper

Place a single layer of sesame seeds on a large plate, and one at a time, press the steaks down on the seeds to coat them on each side.

Place the broccoli and garlic in a large saucepan of water, and cook for 8–10 minutes. Drain, then place in a food processor with the pine nuts, basil, olive oil, and black pepper, and blend to a textured purée.

Heat a drizzle of olive oil in a large, nonstick pan over medium heat. Sear the steaks for a few minutes on each side. Remove from the heat. If you like your steak rare, take the meat out of the pan immediately. If you prefer your meat a little more done, leave it to rest in the hot pan for an additional 5 minutes before serving.

Serve the steaks over a layer of broccoli purée and garnish with a few toasted pine nuts, and fresh basil leaves.

TIP GOOD STEAK REALLY NEEDS TO BE COOKED RARE. DON'T BE AFRAID OF THIS — THE HEAT KILLS ANY BACTERIA, SO JUST USE THE FRESHEST MEAT YOU CAN BUY, AND YOU ARE SET TO GO.

There is another way to cook this: sear the lamb on a hot BBQ for about 3 minutes on each side, then close the barbecue hood, turn off the heat, and leave for about 3 hours. I did this by mistake many years ago when I ran out of coal, and it resulted in the best lamb I have ever tasted. It is how the Greeks cook the lamb dish Kleftiko — slow cooking it so it falls off the bone.

ROAST LEG
OF LAMB

509 calories | 21.9g fat | 10.9g saturates | 1.9g sugar | 0.7g salt | 59.7g protein | 1.5g fiber

Serves 6

4½ lb leg of lamb on
   the bone
4 garlic cloves, thinly
   sliced
6 sprigs of rosemary,
   each cut into 3, plus
   extra for the gravy
2 tablespoons olive oil
freshly ground black
   pepper

for the Greek salad

1 cucumber, chopped into
   chunks
10 cherry tomatoes,
   halved
24 pitted Kalamata
   olives, halved
a handful of salad leaves
a handful of mint leaves
1 tablespoon olive oil
juice of ¼ lemon

Preheat the oven to 400°F.

Place the lamb in a roasting pan, and with a sharp knife, make deep ½-inch cuts in the meat in about 15–20 places. Fill each incision with a slice of garlic and a sprig of rosemary. Drizzle over the olive oil, and massage into the meat.

Cover the lamb with foil, and place in the oven. After 30 minutes, remove the foil, then return the meat to the oven, and cook for another hour.

When ready, lift the meat from the roasting pan and rest on a plate for 10 minutes before serving. To keep the lamb warm, you can cover it with the foil you used before.

To make the salad, place the cucumber, tomatoes, olives, and salad leaves in a bowl, and toss to combine. Scatter the mint leaves over the top, and dress with the oil and lemon.

To make the gravy, place the roasting pan on the stove, and heat up the cooking juices with 4–6 tablespoons water. Add some chopped rosemary and a twist of black pepper, and simmer gently until reduced to a light, flavorsome gravy.

Serve the lamb with the gravy and the fresh Greek salad on the side.

Venison is a meat that is very, very lean, so it's perfect for when you are trying to cut down on fat. If you like your beef cooked rare, prepare venison in the same way — it will be wonderfully tender.

VENISON
ON KALE

602 calories | 32.6g fat | 5g saturates | 2.5g sugar | 0.6g salt | 74g protein | 3g fiber

Serves 4

4 x 10-oz venison
   steaks
freshly ground black
   pepper
3 tablespoons almond oil
   or olive oil
½ white onion, chopped
8 oz kale
1 teaspoon chopped
   capers
juice of ½ lemon
½ cup almonds,
   roughly chopped
½ cup toasted pine nuts
1 tablespoon finely
   chopped flat-leaf
   parsley

Season the steaks with black pepper. Heat 1 tablespoon of the almond or olive oil in a large, nonstick frying pan, and sear the venison steaks over high heat for 3–4 minutes on each side. If you like your meat rare, lift the steaks out of the hot pan immediately, and transfer them to a plate. If you prefer your meat a little more done, leave the meat to rest in the hot pan for an additional 5 minutes.

Meanwhile, heat the remaining oil in a large, nonstick frying pan, and fry the onion over high heat for 3 minutes. Add the kale, and cook for 3–4 minutes, then add the capers, lemon juice, and nuts. Heat for just a minute, tossing to combine.

Serve the venison over the kale with a sprinkling of parsley to garnish.

TIP KALE IS ONE OF THE MOST NUTRITIOUS VEGETABLES YOU CAN EAT — ONE SERVING CONTAINS MORE VITAMIN C THAN AN ORANGE, AND MORE VITAMIN A THAN ANY OTHER LEAFY GREEN.

This dish contains all the best Italian flavors, although obviously the pesto contains no Parmesan cheese! Parmesan is one of the most high-fat cheeses there is and, by eliminating it, you make the pesto guilt-free. There are so many flavors here that you won't miss it one bit.

ROASTED VEGETABLES
WITH PESTO

644 calories | 49.4g fat | 6g saturates | 27.3g sugar | 0.15g salt | 14g protein | 18g fiber

Serves 4

1 butternut squash, peeled and quartered
14 oz cauliflower florets
12 oz carrots, peeled and sliced
14 oz Brussels sprouts
1 red onion, peeled and quartered
4 tablespoons olive oil
freshly ground black pepper

for the pesto
12–16 fresh basil leaves
scant ½ cup olive oil
2 garlic cloves, peeled
¾ cup toasted pine nuts

Preheat the oven to 425°F.

Place all the vegetables in a roasting pan, and toss with the olive oil, and season with black pepper. Cook in the oven for about 40 minutes, tossing thoroughly at the halfway point.

Meanwhile, blend all the pesto ingredients in a food processor, and set aside.

Remove the vegetables from the oven, dress with the pesto and serve.

TIP IF YOU LIKE YOUR SPROUTS A LITTLE CRUNCHY, ADD THEM WHEN YOU TOSS THE VEGETABLES HALFWAY THROUGH.

Cauliflower is delicious in curry dishes and makes a great vegetarian option. You can always spice this up with a little more fiery chili if you like.

CAULIFLOWER
AND MUSHROOM CURRY

326 calories | 27g fat | 16.5g saturates | 5.9g sugar | trace salt | 9.9g protein | 5.2g fiber

Serves 4

1 head of cauliflower, broken into florets
3 tablespoons olive oil
freshly ground black pepper
1 large onion, chopped
3 garlic cloves, crushed
9 oz button mushrooms
1-inch piece of fresh ginger, grated
1 tablespoon ground coriander
1 tablespoon ground cumin
1 tablespoon garam masala
1 tablespoon chili powder (or more, to taste)
14 fl oz light coconut milk
a handful of fresh cilantro, chopped

Preheat the oven to 425°F.

In a roasting pan, toss the cauliflower florets in 2 tablespoons of the olive oil, and season with pepper. Roast for 25 minutes, tossing occasionally until the cauliflower starts to brown. Remove from the oven, and set aside.

In a wide, shallow pan, fry the onion in the remaining tablespoon of olive oil over high heat for 3–4 minutes. Add the garlic, mushrooms, and ginger, and cook for another minute, stirring.

Stir in the spices, and cook for a minute, then add the coconut milk. Season to taste. Bring to a boil, then stir in the cauliflower. Reduce the heat, cover the pan, and cook for about 5 minutes on low heat. Serve with plenty of fresh cilantro.

TIP IF YOU'D LIKE TO MAKE THIS DISH FAT-FREE, SIMPLY REPLACE THE COCONUT MILK WITH VEGETABLE STOCK.

This is perfect for when you have vegetarian friends over for dinner. It's pretty simple to make, but looks impressive, as if you've been in the kitchen preparing it for hours!

EGGPLANT STACKS WITH HERB OIL

412 calories | 40.4g fat | 4.8g saturates | 7.2g sugar | 0.1g salt | 5.1g protein | 5.5g fiber

Serves 4

6 tablespoons olive oil
2 large eggplants, sliced into 1-inch thick rounds
2 tablespoons sun-dried tomato paste
2 garlic cloves, crushed
⅔ cup pine nuts
20–25 cherry tomatoes, halved
a handful of fresh basil, roughly chopped
freshly ground black pepper

for the herb oil

scant ¼ cup olive oil
handful of fresh herbs
1 garlic clove, finely chopped

Heat 2 tablespoons of the olive oil in a heavy, nonstick pan, and fry the eggplant slices over medium heat for about 4 minutes on each side.

Meanwhile, place the sun-dried tomato paste, garlic, pine nuts, and cherry tomatoes in a mixing bowl, and pour over the remaining olive oil. Toss everything together, and add the basil.

Now layer up the eggplant like a tower. Lay the largest slice down as the base, and spread a spoonful of the tomato mixture over the top, then add another eggplant slice, and continue to layer up until you have a stack about 4–5 slices high.

Blend all the herb oil ingredients together in a bowl.

Serve the eggplant towers with a drizzle of herb oil around the edge of the plate, and a twist or two of black pepper.

If you miss potatoes, this is the answer. To me, butternut squash is the best vegetable you can have on the Paleo diet — roast it, mash it, make soups with it, and stir-fry it, and you'll never have a carb craving again.

BUTTERNUT RATATOUILLE

194 calories | 11.7g fat | 1.7g saturates | 12.7g sugar | 0.1g salt | 3.4g protein | 6.7g fiber

Serves 4

1 small butternut squash, peeled, halved, and chopped into small chunks
4 tablespoons olive oil
freshly ground black pepper
1 onion, finely chopped
1 eggplant, chopped into cubes
1 tablespoon tomato paste
2 garlic cloves, crushed
2 large tomatoes, seeded and diced
a handful of fresh basil, shredded

Preheat the oven to 425°F.

Place the butternut squash in a roasting pan, and toss in 2 tablespoons of the olive oil. Season with black pepper, and cook for 25 minutes, tossing halfway through.

Meanwhile, heat 1 tablespoon of the olive oil in a large sauté pan and sweat the onions for 2 minutes, then add the eggplant, and cook, tossing for 5 minutes.

Add the remaining olive oil, tomato paste, garlic, tomatoes, and roasted squash. Stir all the ingredients to mix thoroughly, and cook for an additional 4–5 minutes.

Serve hot or warm, with a garnish of fresh basil, and an extra twist of black pepper.

TIP EGGPLANTS ARE FULL OF DIETARY FIBER, SO WILL KEEP YOU FEELING FULL, AND STOP YOU BEING TEMPTED TO SNACK.

For me, this is the best dish in the book. Whenever I feel a carb craving coming on, this is the recipe I reach for. I have not stopped making it since the first attempt and I hope you will try it, and love it too.

SPAGHETTI ACORN SQUASH

279 calories | 12.3g fat | 1.8g saturates | 22.2g sugar | 0.2g salt | 8g protein | 11g fiber

Serves 2

2 tablespoons olive oil
1 acorn squash, halved and peeled into long ribbons
2 zucchini, peeled into long ribbons
2 garlic cloves, crushed
6 oz cherry tomatoes, halved
2 tablespoons sun-dried tomato paste
freshly ground black pepper
a handful of fresh basil leaves

Heat 1 tablespoon of the olive oil in a large, nonstick pan, and add the squash. Toss over medium heat for 3 minutes, then add the zucchini and cook for an additional 2–3 minutes.

Add the remaining olive oil, plus the garlic, tomatoes, and tomato paste, and cook for 2–3 minutes, stirring, to coat. Reduce the heat to low, and toss.

Remove the pan from the heat, and turn the contents onto a plate. Season with black pepper, tear over the fresh basil and serve.

TIP YOU REALLY WON'T MISS CARB-HEAVY PASTA ONE BIT WHEN YOU'VE TRIED THESE LOVELY RIBBONS OF SQUASH — THEY HOLD A SAUCE FANTASTICALLY WELL, SO TRY THEM WITH ALL SORTS OF TOPPINGS.

DESSERTS

Some desserts leave you feeling guilty and bloated, but this one does neither. It has a wonderful Mediterranean feel about it, and makes you want to dine al fresco and savor every bite.

BROILED FRUIT WITH CINNAMON AND HONEY

193 calories | 3.2g fat | 2.5g saturates | 38.4g sugar | 0g salt | 3.7g protein | 6.6g fiber

Serves 4

4 nectarines, halved and pitted

6 figs, halved

4 plums, halved and pitted

2 apples, quartered and cored

1 cinnamon stick, broken

2 tablespoons raw honey

1 tablespoon coconut oil

2 teaspoons ground cinnamon

Preheat the broiler to a moderate heat.

Place all the fruit in a roasting pan and mix together. Tuck the pieces of cinnamon stick into any gaps.

In a small saucepan, heat the honey and coconut oil together. Drizzle this syrup over the fruit, then place the roasting pan under the broiler, and cook for 3–4 minutes, until the fruits caramelize and darken.

Serve in bowls with a sprinkling of ground cinnamon.

TIP USE WHATEVER FRUITS ARE IN SEASON FOR THIS DISH — PLUMS, APPLES, BLACKBERRIES, RASPBERRIES, PINEAPPLE, ETC. — ALL ARE DELICIOUS!

This pudding will take you back to your childhood,
I guarantee you. It's the perfect thing to whip up at a moment's notice.

BANANA PUDDING

235 calories | 10.2g fat | 9.1g saturates | 30.6g sugar | 0g salt | 2.4g protein | 1.8g fiber

Serves 4

4 ripe bananas
14 fl oz light coconut milk
1 tablespoon raw honey
fresh mint, to garnish

Place the bananas, coconut milk, and honey in a blender, and blitz until smooth.

Divide the mixture between 4 ramekins, and chill in the fridge for 30 minutes.

Serve with a sprig of fresh mint.

This is a great dessert that always reminds me of Thailand. It
tastes very indulgent, but in fact, there's nothing to feel guilty about at all.

CARAMEL BANANAS

276 calories | 9.9g fat | 1.9g saturates | 41.7g sugar | 0.3g salt | 3.9g protein | 3g fiber

Serves 4

4 ripe bananas, peeled
1 tablespoon coconut oil
14 fl oz light coconut milk
3 tablespoons raw honey
3 tablespoons sesame seeds

With a sharp knife, thickly slice the bananas on an angle.

Heat the oil in a heavy, nonstick sauté pan over high heat, and cook the bananas for about 2 minutes.

Add the coconut milk and honey, reduce the heat, and simmer for 5 minutes.

Spoon the bananas into small bowls, and serve with a sprinkling of sesame seeds.

As a child, I loved going to Chinese restaurants, as their sesame, apple and banana desserts were always my favorite. This dish is a far healthier option, and yet it still reminds me a little of those fantastic childhood flavors.

FRIED CINNAMON BANANAS

274 calories | 14g fat | 12g saturates | 33.7g sugar | 0g salt | 2g protein | 3.3g fiber

Serves 4

4 ripe bananas, peeled
3 tablespoons coconut oil
2 tablespoons raw honey
1 teaspoon ground cinnamon
4 tablespoons flaked coconut

Using a sharp knife, quarter each banana lengthwise (so you have 4 long strips).

Heat the oil in a frying pan over low heat, and cook the banana slices for 2–3 minutes.

Lift the bananas out of the pan, and drain on paper towels. Discard the oil from the pan.

Return the bananas to the pan, and place over medium heat. Add the honey and cinnamon, and toss to coat, cooking for about a minute, until golden. Add the coconut flakes and serve.

TIP NUMEROUS STUDIES HAVE SHOWN THAT CINNAMON IS VERY EFFECTIVE FOR REGULATING BLOOD SUGAR. IT ALSO ADDS A DELICIOUS FLAVOR TO ALMOST ANY COOKED FRUIT, SO ADD A DUSTING TO PLUMS, BANANAS, PINEAPPLE, APPLES... YOU NAME IT.

This is the best way to have ice cream on the Paleo diet.
However, be aware that, as you are not using cream, the coconut milk
can crystallize in the freezer to make a more granita-type ice. For a creamier,
more mousse-like texture, try freezing for just 30 minutes.

COCONUT AND ALMOND

ICE CREAM

319 calories | 25.7g fat | 11.9g saturates | 14g sugar | 0g salt | 6.4g protein | 0.5g fiber

Serves 4

¾ cup almonds
1 pint light coconut milk
3 tablespoons raw honey

Place the almonds in a ziplock bag, and bash them with a rolling pin until they resemble rough crumbs.

Mix the almond crumbs in a bowl with the coconut milk. In a saucepan, warm the honey over low heat, and then drizzle into the bowl, stirring to combine.

Pour the mixture into a freezer-proof container, and freeze for at least 2 hours before serving.

COCONUT AND MANGO

ICE CREAM

243 calories | 19g fat | 17.1g saturates | 14.9g sugar | 0g salt | 2g protein | 3.2g fiber

Serves 4

1 mango, peeled and
   chopped
2 tablespoons raw honey
1 pint light coconut milk
2 cups flaked coconut
fresh mint leaves,
   to serve

Place the mango in a blender with the honey, and blitz until smooth.

In a bowl, combine the coconut milk with the coconut flakes. Pour in the mango purée, reserving a little for later, and stir to combine.

Pour the mixture into a freezer-proof container, and freeze for at least 2 hours.

Serve in a martini glass, drizzled with the reserved mango purée, and garnished with a fresh mint leaf.

Pineapple is full of natural sugar, so when you combine it with honey and heat, you get a wonderful, sticky, caramelized result.

BROILED

PINEAPPLE

115 calories | 0.3g fat | 0g saturates | 28.6g sugar | 0g salt | 0.8g protein | 2.8g fiber

Serves 4

juice of 1 lemon
1 pineapple, peeled
   and cut into wedges
   or slices
3 tablespoons raw honey
a dusting of ground
   cinnamon
a few mint leaves, finely
   chopped

Squeeze the lemon over the pineapple pieces so they don't discolor. Drizzle over the honey, and toss so it is thoroughly coated.

Heat a griddle pan over medium heat, and when hot, add the pineapple and griddle for 4–5 minutes on each side until it caramelizes.

Dust the pineapple with ground cinnamon to serve, and scatter over the chopped mint to garnish.

TIP SWEET AND DELICIOUS, PINEAPPLE IS PACKED FULL OF NUTRIENTS — FULL OF ANTIOXIDANT PROTECTION AND IMMUNE SUPPORT.

I don't believe that diets should take out all the enjoyment from life, and so this recipe means you can still enjoy cake, and not break any Paleo rules. It's perfect with a cup of morning or afternoon herbal tea.

LEMON
POUND CAKE

412 calories | 33.1g fat | 13.7g saturates | 9.7g sugar | 0.2g salt | 13.5g protein | 6.9g fiber

Serves 6

6 tablespoons coconut oil,
   plus extra for greasing
4 tablespoons raw honey
2 scant cups
   almond flour
⅔ cup coconut flour
4 eggs
zest and juice of 1 lemon
   (or 1 teaspoon
   lemon extract)

Preheat the oven to 350°F, and lightly oil a round 9-inch deep cake pan.

Place a small saucepan over low heat, and melt the coconut oil and honey. (You can also do this in the microwave for about 30 seconds.)

In a large mixing bowl, combine the almond and coconut flours. Add the melted honey and oil mixture, eggs, lemon zest and juice, and whisk together to mix well.

Pour the cake mix into the prepared pan, and bake for 30 minutes, or until a thin skewer inserted into the center of the cake comes out clean.

Remove the cake from the oven, and leave in the pan until completely cold. Turn out onto a plate, and serve with a cup of herbal tea.

TIP ALMOND FLOUR AND COCONUT FLOUR ARE EASY TO BAKE WITH — THEY'RE JUST A LITTLE DRIER THAN REGULAR FLOUR, SO YOU NEED A LITTLE MORE EGG TO BIND EVERYTHING TOGETHER.

Carrot cake made its debut in the 1960s, although carrot has been used as a sweetener since medieval times. In any case, it is very appropriate to use it in this way to make this wonderfully tasty Paleo cake.

CARROT
CAKE

531 calories | 38.1g fat | 17.4g saturates | 24.1g sugar | 0.4g salt | 16.5g protein | 11g fiber

Serves 6

6 tablespoons melted coconut oil, plus extra for greasing
4 tablespoons maple syrup
1⅔ cups almond flour
⅔ cup coconut flour
1 teaspoon freshly grated nutmeg
1 teaspoon ground cinnamon
3½ fl oz prune juice
6 eggs, beaten
1 teaspoon vanilla extract
4 large carrots, peeled, and finely grated
⅔ cup shredded dry coconut
scant ½ cup raisins

Preheat the oven to 350°F, and lightly oil an 8¼ x 4¼-inch loaf pan.

Place a small saucepan over low heat, and melt the coconut oil and maple syrup. (You can also do this in the microwave for about 30 seconds.)

In a large mixing bowl or food processor, combine all the remaining ingredients, and mix together well.

Pour the cake mix into the prepared pan, and bake for 40–50 minutes, or until a thin skewer inserted into the center of the cake comes out clean.

Remove the cake from the oven, and leave in the pan until completely cold. Turn out onto a plate, and serve with a cup of herbal tea.

This is a tried-and-tested traditional dessert that has been tweaked only slightly to substitute the sugar for raw honey, so it's all good on the Paleo diet. The lime zest is a lovely addition, and cleans the palate at the end of the meal.

POACHED PEARS

138 calories | 0.2g fat | 0g saturates | 35.3g sugar | 0g salt | 0.7g protein | 5.g fiber

Serves 4

juice and zest of 2 limes
8 small pears, peeled, with stems still on
3 cups water
4 tablespoons raw honey
a few drops of vanilla extract

Pour the lime juice over the pears to stop them from turning brown.

Transfer the pears and lime juice to a large saucepan. Sit the pears upright and cover with the water and honey. Bring the water to a boil, and simmer for about 10 minutes, or until the pears are tender all the way through when pierced with a skewer — cooking times will vary depending on the ripeness of your fruit.

Remove the pears with a slotted spoon and arrange on a serving plate.

Add the vanilla extract to the poaching liquid, and boil to reduce by half, stirring occasionally. Set aside to cool.

Serve each pear with the cooled syrup and a garnish of lime zest.

TIP PEARS ARE FULL OF FIBER (24% OF YOUR RDA) SO KEEP YOUR DIGESTIVE SYSTEM IN SHIP-SHAPE CONDITION.

INDEX

ACKNOWLEDGMENTS

I am extremely grateful to my nephew, Alexander Green, a recent graduate from Oxford who, with his valuable research, has made a huge contribution to this book.

It has been such a pleasure to work with Kyle Books again. Kyle has always seen that my passion is creating healthy food that is full of flavor. After losing 64lbs myself many years ago, I know what a struggle it can be, and so I love to hear feedback from readers about their weight-loss progress. Please follow me on Facebook: Chef Daniel Green